❧ COFFEE & CAKE ❧

RICK RODGERS

The Turkey Cookbook

365 Ways to Cook Hamburger and Other Ground Meats

Mr. Pasta's Healthy Pasta Cookbook

Fondue

Slow Cooker Ready & Waiting

The Baker's Dozen Cookbook (ed.)

Dip It

Thanksgiving 101

Christmas 101

Summer Gatherings

Autumn Gatherings

Winter Gatherings

Spring Gatherings

Tea and Cookies

Kaffeehaus

coffee & cake

Enjoy the Perfect
Cup of Coffee—with Dozens
of Delectable Recipes for Café Treats

RICK RODGERS

PHOTOGRAPHS BY BEN FINK

WILLIAM MORROW
An Imprint of HarperCollins*Publishers*

HarperCollins books may be purchased for educational, business, or sales promotional use. For information please write: Special Markets Department, HarperCollins Publishers, 10 East 53rd Street, New York, NY 10022.

FIRST EDITION

Designed by Paula Russell Szafranski

Library of Congress Cataloging-in-Publication Data

Rodgers, Rick, 1953–
   Coffee and cake : enjoy the perfect cup of coffee—with dozens of delectable recipes for café treats / Rick Rodgers; photographs by Ben Fink. —1st ed.
      p. cm.
   Includes index.
   ISBN 978-0-06-193832-0
1. Coffee brewing. 2. Coffee. 3. Cake. I. Title.
   TX817.C6R634 2010
   641.3'373—dc22

                     2009052093

10 11 12 13 14 OV/RRD 10 9 8 7 6 5 4 3 2 1

ACKNOWLEDGMENTS

Coffee and cake have been a constant in my life. The same can be said of many of the people who show up again and again to help me produce a cookbook. It is my name on the book, but a cookbook is really a group effort.

Thanks to John Simmons, who introduced me to his colleagues at illycaffè, Italian-based purveyor of extraordinary coffee. Myra Fiori and Laura Bachman invited me to attend the company's Università del Caffè, an intensive course on coffee production and service that was an important source of information for this book. I must also thank John's wife and my fellow cookbook writer, Marie Simmons, for putting this chain of events in motion. And a very special tip of my coffee mug to Melissa Palmer of Krups, Group SEB, for the generous use of Krups's excellent coffeemakers in photography.

At William Morrow, I consider myself very lucky to work with Cassie Jones, an editor who truly collaborates with an author to make the book the best it can be. Jessica Deputato, Cassie's assistant, is invaluable to the bookmaking process. David Sweeney has been a longtime supporter of my work, and I am extremely grateful for his input along the way. I am also beholden to Sonia Greenbaum, my excellent copy editor, and Paula Russell Szafranski, the book's talented designer. And I lift my cappuccino in thanks to Dee Dee Bartolo and Adam Rochind for their work to publicize my books.

At home, a terrific group of friends and family worked together to create *Coffee and Cake*. Ben Fink is a fine photographer who has become a valued friend. This is our eighth book together. Diane Kniss has been my irreplaceable assistant for twenty-five wonderful years, which must be some kind of record in the volatile food industry. (And, yes, we were very young when we met!) Susan Ginsburg has been my tireless agent and dear friend for even longer, as hard as that is to believe. Thanks so much, too, to Susan's assistant, Bethany Strout. Skip Dye and Steven King were characteristically generous in lending me many gorgeous pieces from their tabletop collection. And, as always, Patrick Fisher was our biggest fan.

This book is dedicated to my dear friend, the late Irene Jenkins, who started educating me about coffee when she was my translator and guide in Vienna for another coffee-related book, *Kaffeehaus*. Irene and I shared countless cups of coffee and slices of cake during our research, and her kindness, warmth, and range of knowledge, from art history to coffee-making, were inspiring.

CONTENTS

❧ COFFEE & CAKE ❧

INTRODUCTION

When I was growing up, coffee and cake were almost inseparable. Certainly we drank coffee in its most familiar form, on its own to jumpstart the day or as an afternoon pick-me-up. But my most vivid memories are of coffee paired with cake, appearing together at special family gatherings. From birthday parties to baby showers to weddings, homemade cakes were carefully constructed and proudly served, always with a steaming pot of coffee.

My mother's family came from Liechtenstein, so their attitude toward coffee and cake was informed by the Old World coffee culture, with its cozy coffeehouses and luscious pastries. Even the American tradition of the coffee klatsch, an at-home gathering with coffee and sweets, had its beginnings in mid-nineteenth-century Germany. But the love of coffee and cake is hardly restricted to German-speaking people.

Today, virtually every American town has a coffeehouse of some kind, either a satellite of a mega-chain or a privately owned shop, selling many varieties of coffee beans and a wide range of beverages. Italian espresso-based coffee drinks have become commonplace, but so have coffee beverages from Vietnam or Thailand, readily purchased (with appropriate sweets) at Asian restaurants. Coffee has long been a part of the American social experience, but now that experience has a more international feeling, light years beyond the dented percolator on the back of the stove. For hundreds of years, the caffeine in coffee has served as a stimulant to encourage lively conversation at any gathering, and where there is coffee, cake is usually close by. Cakes are meant to be shared. Even the most gluttonous of gluttons would be hard-pressed to bake a cake and eat it alone.

Coffee and Cake shows how to prepare these two separate, yet inseparable, components at their very best in your home. Coffee is a very complex subject, and there are innumerable varieties of cakes, but this book focuses on the essentials. First, the Coffee Primer teaches the basics of how to choose beans to suit your personal taste and make a better cup of coffee—you'll learn some fascinating historical facts about coffee along the way, too. The next chapter shows a range of coffee beverages, both hot and iced. Then, a second primer lays out the groundwork for baking wonderful cakes time after time, followed by cake recipes designed to be savored with coffee. You can choose simple and rustic cakes for serving at a coffee klatsch, fun cupcakes for both kids and grown-ups, American-style cakes that are sure to bring back memories of old-fashioned flavors, and elaborate creations worthy of a European café.

So, the next time you invite friends for a chat over a cup of coffee and a slice of cake, turn to *Coffee and Cake* for ways to make both the best you've ever served.

A COFFEE PRIMER

*I*t's easy to take coffee for granted. For many of us, drinking a cup of the dark, aromatic brew is at the very least an everyday occurrence. However, the steps taken to get the coffee in your mug involve countless people, usually thousands of miles away.

The economics of coffee are staggering. After oil, green (unroasted) coffee beans are the second most traded commodity in the world, literally providing the grounds for the approximately 500 billion cups brewed annually. Depending on the source, it is estimated that anywhere from 60 to 120 million people rely on coffee for their livelihood—and whatever the true number, that's a lot of people. Growing, harvesting, and processing coffee are extremely labor intensive, as these numbers show.

However, today's consumers are hardly taking coffee for granted. More and more coffee lovers are choosing their coffee very carefully, paying close attention to the source of the bean, the darkness of the roast, and, with the impact of the fair-trade and sustainable-agriculture movements, the political implications of their purchase. This primer will walk you through the basics of coffee, from its history to its agriculture, and then on to its preparation in your home. You will learn to make sense of some of the less familiar words at your local coffee purveyor—what is Organic SHG Chiapas Coffee, anyway? You will end up with newfound appreciation for your cup of java.

A SHORT HISTORY OF COFFEE 🍃

While it is difficult to pinpoint its exact origin, most experts cite Ethiopia as the source of the arabica coffee plant (the more important of the two major commercial species). As it is one of the few plants that contain caffeine, the natives must have noticed the effect it had on their wakefulness. The berries and leaves were boiled to make a kind of tea, and the berries were mixed with animal fat to make a kind of prehistoric energy bar.

From there it migrated to modern-day Yemen, just across a narrow strait from the coffee-producing area of Africa. Coffee, as a stimulating but not intoxicating substitute for forbidden alcoholic beverages, became an important part of Islamic life. The Arabs learned to roast the beans to improve their flavor. Most of the words we use for coffee are from Muslim cultures. The Turkish *khaveh* is in turn derived from the Arabic *qahweh*. Mocha is named for the Yemenite port on the Red Sea (today's Al-Mokka) that was the Arabian coffee's major distribution point. (The term mocha has nothing to do with chocolate, although some people may find a hint of naturally occurring cacao flavor in Arabian coffee beans.) It's also possible that the word evolved from the Kaffee region of Ethiopia, one of the areas where coffee was first cultivated.

Coffee remained an exclusively Muslim beverage until the late 1500s, when Venetian traders began to bring the beans to Italy. For various reasons (including its Muslim heritage and its inexplicable effect on the nervous system), coffee was originally considered an evil drink until no less a personage than Pope Clement II tried the beverage and deemed it fit for Christians to drink. And drink it they did. From Venice, it spread like wildfire throughout Europe, first to the courts, and then to the populace. Following a terrible siege of Vienna in 1683, the departing Turks left behind bags of coffee beans and established a place for coffee in Austrian culture.

Coffeehouses, especially those in London, became much more than just venues where locals could sample this new beverage. (In the Old World, there was a difference between a coffeehouse, which specialized in serving coffee and tea with light meals sold as a mere convenience, and a café, which offered more substantial food. The line is blurred today.) Charles II unsuccessfully tried to close them as "places where the disaffected met and spread scandalous reports concerning the conduct of His Majesty and his Ministers." Entire cults developed around coffeehouses and their habitués, a practice that only weakened when World War II changed the entire fabric of European culture.

The first American coffeehouse opened in Boston in 1669. The British had a virtual monopoly on the tea trade and controlled its price, usually unfairly. After the Boston Tea Party in 1773, drinking tea became an unpopular pro-British act, and coffee, which could be imported directly from Caribbean farms, made inroads in America's beverage habits. When another embargo affected tea trade during the War of 1812, coffee became the American beverage of choice. Our collective coffee culture includes coffee shops, cafeterias, and the Bohemian urban cafés of the 1950s. The latter carried on the tradition of being hot spots for political protest, with music added to spread the protesters' messages. Dare I say that without coffee there would be no Bob Dylan?

Various trends affected the rise of American coffee consumption, both in and out of the home. First, technology vastly improved coffeemakers beyond the familiar percolator, which usually burned the coffee but didn't stop people from drinking it. Both the automatic drip coffee machine and the personal espresso machine irrevocably altered how Americans make coffee in their kitchens. Better machines inspired consumers to buy better beans. Coffee retailers selling top-quality beans began to appear outside of urban areas and, ultimately, online. Outside the home, the proliferation of coffeehouses, both as outposts of mega-chains and individually managed cafés, has made getting artfully prepared European coffee drinks an everyday occurrence.

Coffee Talk

Like wine, coffee has its own terminology to describe its flavor and other characteristics.

Also like wine, it may seem useful to talk about coffee in broad terms based on its place of origin. However, just as there are many different grapes with various attributes in Bordeaux or Burgundy, keep in mind that there are many microclimates in coffee-growing countries that make it difficult to speak in generalizations. Nonetheless, it is done. While these descriptions are somewhat subjective, they are more or less standard throughout the industry.

Acidity: Also known as "brightness," the lively tartness found in the best coffees, especially those grown in highland regions.

Aroma: The fragrance of brewed coffee.

Body: The perceived weight of brewed coffee in your mouth, which can range from light and thin to heavy and syrupy.

Earthy: A flavor reminiscent of soil, and used in a positive way to describe Indonesian coffees, and as a negative in other varieties.

Mellow: Denotes coffee with low to medium acidity.

Mild: A well-balanced coffee without any overriding flavors.

Spicy: Used when the natural aroma of a brewed coffee is reminiscent of a particular spice, such as cinnamon.

Winy: Some Arabian and African coffees have this characteristic, similar to the fruity flavor of red wine.

THE COFFEE BELT ❧

The evergreen coffee plant must be grown between the Tropics of Cancer and Capricorn in rainy, frost-free areas (a drought or frost can wreak havoc on the coffee industry). It takes three to five years to establish a coffee plant (often called a tree, although it is pruned to bush height for ease of bean picking), and it will produce for about fifteen years, after which it must be replaced.

Coffee beans are actually the seeds of the plant's fruit, which are called "cherries" because of their round shape and red color. The cherries do not ripen at the same time, so a picker may have to go back four or five times during a harvest to gather all the fruit, but each tree will only yield about one to ten pounds of cherries, depending on the age of the tree and the quality of the particular growing season. There are two beans per cherry; a cherry with a single bean is called a "peaberry."

The two major coffee species for commercial use are arabica (*Coffea arabica*) and robusta (*Coffea canephora* var. *robusta*). Arabica, which produces the highest-quality coffee, must be grown in rich, preferably volcanic, soil at elevations 2,500 to 6,000 feet above sea level. Arabica accounts for more than 70 percent of all coffee production. Some arabica varieties do best when protected from harsh sunlight, and are called shade-grown. Robusta is a heartier species, hence its name. It is less susceptible to disease than arabica and can be grown at lower altitudes, but robusta also makes a more bitter, harsher brew. For this reason, robusta is usually blended with arabica or used as the main bean in canned or instant brands. Some people consider robusta no more than filler in a blend, but others believe it is a useful flavor booster to arabica. However, a large producer recently removed all the robusta from its canned blend so it could be marketed as "all-arabica" (and also because it got grief from conservationists over the nonsustainable manner in which the Vietnamese robusta beans were being grown). There are few robusta coffees that are sold unblended. On the plus side, it is used in espresso blends, as it helps form the *crema* layer on top of an espresso.

Over seventy countries grow coffee, and they can be grouped into three major regions. *The Americas* include Brazil, Colombia, Guatemala, Honduras, and Mexico, as well as such coffee-producing Caribbean islands as Jamaica and Haiti. These coffees are characterized by lively, bright flavors with moderate body. The coffees of *Africa* and *Arabia* (such as Arabian Mocha, Ethiopia, Kenya, Malawi, Tanzania, and Zimbabwe) often have spicy notes. *Asian* and *Pacific* coffees (Indonesia, Java, Sumatra, and Vietnam, among others) are known for moderate acidity, earthy flavors, and full body.

Coffee can be labeled for sale to the consumer in a number of ways. Usually, the country of origin comes first, followed by the specific area where the bean was harvested. An example of this would be Ethiopian Harrar. Additional modifiers may include the processing style (dry, wet or washed, or semiwashed), the size of the bean (for example, Maragogipes refers to mutant "elephant-size" beans grown in some Latin American areas), or whether the bean is arabica or robusta. Sometimes the kind of roast becomes the predominant identifier (such as Viennese Roast, without mention of the beans). You may also find out whether the coffee is from a single estate or farm, or if it contains just one type of bean or a blend. As you become familiar with the terms, a formerly confusing label will become comprehensible.

The following countries are the top ten coffee producers in the world in descending order, with the approximate number of bags (each bag weighs 132 pounds/60 kilos) harvested in 2008:

Brazil (45,992,000 bags) is the top producer of coffee beans, providing about one-third of the global supply. In fact, the industry is so dependent on the success of the Brazilian crop that just the threat of a destructive frost can affect the commodity's price. Another way to illustrate Brazil's superior position is the fact that it produces more than the next five coffee-crop countries combined. It grows mostly arabica beans to be blended with other beans, although some excellent estate-grown varietals may make it to your coffee purveyor. Bourbon Santos, with bright notes and a fruity flavor, is a good bet for a single-bean (unblended) coffee. (Bourbon is an old arabica strain originally grown on the French colonial island now called Réunion, and Santos is a busy Brazilian port.)

There is a delightfully sexy story about how coffee came to be planted in Brazil. In the early 1700s, the coffee-growing regions jealously guarded their crops. A Brazilian politician was sent to French Guinea to solve a dispute, and while he was there, he seduced the governor's wife, perhaps with a plan to swipe some Guinean coffee seeds. If that was true, it worked, for she did hide coffee cuttings in a *bon voyage* bouquet. These cuttings became the progenitors of Brazil's coffee industry.

Vietnam (16,000,000 bags) can trace its coffee ancestry to the French plantations established during the colonial period. The arabica crops were destroyed by a blight of coffee rust, and were replaced by hardier robusta plants, which now comprise almost 90 percent of production. You will rarely find estate-grown Vietnamese coffee, as most of it becomes inexpensive canned or instant coffee. Conservationists say that Vietnam's rapid rise to second place in the global production of coffee is at the expense of basic ecological concerns.

Colombia (10,500,000 bags) has the perfect environment for arabica coffee plants, with a mountainous terrain and a good amount of rainfall that makes irrigation unnecessary. Most of the crop is planted with banana and rubber trees to provide shade. The three best-known coffee regions are Medellín, Armenia, and Manizales, which form the acronym MAM found on most exported bags of Colombian coffee. These coffees are known for their full body and moderate acidity. Bucamaranga is another highly regarded coffee, with an even softer, less acidic profile than the MAM varieties. In addition to producing consistently high-quality coffee, Colombia knows how to market it. The fictional character Juan Valdez put a face on the Colombian coffee industry, and in 2005 was noted as the most recognizable advertising icon of the year.

Ethiopia (6,133,000 bags), coffee's birthplace, maintains a strong position in global coffee production, and the Ethiopian coffee industry provides over twelve million jobs. The Ethiopian coffee ceremony, where coffee is meticulously roasted and brewed, is performed three times a day in areas that retain the traditional lifestyle. Ethiopian coffee is famed for its distinctive flavors, from the winy, fruity Harrar to the more delicate Yergacheffe. To protect their unique characteristics, the beans are never dark-roasted, a process that caramelizes the bean and changes its flavor.

Indonesia (5,823,000 bags) is the first place where coffee was cultivated outside of Islamic countries. The industry was started by the Dutch in the 1700s on the island of Java (which became a nickname for coffee itself). The other islands providing most of the coffee crop are

Sumatra, Sulawesi (formerly called Celebes, the name under which some Indonesian coffee is still sold), and Flores. Ninety percent of the crop is robusta, but the arabica beans that make up the balance are of very high quality. You may come across aged Indonesian beans, labeled "Old Government" or "Old Brown," which have been carefully stored and make a thick, almost syrupy brew with sweet notes. Otherwise, try Mandheling or Ankola as examples of full-bodied Sumatrans, Celebes Kalossi for a rich Sulawesi, or the classic Mocha Java, a familiar blend of Yemenite and Indonesian beans.

Mexico (4,650,000 bags) grows its coffee on more than 100,000 small farms. Most of the beans are arabica, and the best ones are from the highlands and graded *altura* ("high-grown" in Spanish) or SHG (Strictly High-Grown). Regions known for great beans include Chiapas, Oaxaca, and Coatapec. There is a high proportion of organic or fair-trade Mexican coffee, grown under standards that monitor the crop-growing methods and the quality of life of the farmers.

India (4,610,000 bags) has entered the specialty coffee business only over the last ten years or so. Before that, the industry was nationalized, and all of the beans were blended together and sold by the government. Now that the farmers are free to grow and market what they wish, some fine single-bean arabicas are being grown (about 60 percent of the crop is robusta). Some Indian coffees are purposely monsooned, aged in a special way to mimic the traditional shipping by sail, where the coffee acquired a specific wild flavor from long exposure to humidity. You might like to try coffee beans from Mysore or Malabar.

Peru (4,102,000 bags) is another country where the coffee is mostly grown on over 110,000 small farms by peasants. The conditions are difficult, if not impossible: picking beans from plants grown on steep mountainsides while dealing with antigovernment guerrillas and drug lords. Peruvian wholesalers also noticed that organic beans sold at a premium, so many farmers quickly changed to organic growing methods—too quickly to be true, some say. Although there are conscientious wholesalers and fair-trade cooperatives working to improve the situation, many coffee experts are cynical about Peru's commitment to organic coffee.

Honduras (3,833,000 bags) produces lots of good coffee that mostly ends up in blends. It doesn't have single-bean or farm-specific coffees, but your purveyor may unearth something special during his or her travels.

Guatemala (3,370,000 bags) continues to grow old strains of coffee plants instead of the newer high-yield, low-flavor plants that other countries use to increase their harvest. Therefore, the best coffee is the equivalent to an "old vine" wine. The coffee is grown both on large *haciendas* (ranches) and small mountainside plots. Two coffees worth trying are from Huehuetenango (especially the SHB, or Strictly Hard Bean grade, harvested from the highest of the highlands) and Antigua.

PROCESSING &

Collecting the coffee cherries from their bushes remains a labor intensive job that is done by hand so the picker can determine the ripeness of the fruit. Some large plantations have mechanical harvesters, but these are mostly farms that are planted on flat terrain, as the machines would be difficult to operate on a mountainside. While a human picker can harvest anywhere from 100 to 200 pounds of cherries a day, only 20 percent of the weight is actually the coffee bean, and the rest will be discarded during processing.

There are three different methods for processing coffee beans. Dry processing is the traditional method, practiced in countries with reliably sunny weather. The cherries are spread out on patios, raked to keep them from fermenting, and dried in the sun over a period of about four weeks. If it rains, the beans must be covered. Coffee beans processed by the dry method are often labeled "natural" or "unwashed."

In wet processing, on the day of harvesting, the cherries are crushed to loosen the skin and pulp covering the beans, then the pulp is washed away with water. The beans are then fermented to help remove any clinging pulp, and dried in the sun or by mechanical means. Coffee processed by this method is sometimes labeled "washed."

Brazil has developed the hybrid semiwashed process for many of their beans. By this procedure, the cherries are pulped, but the mucilage is not washed away and allowed to dry on the beans. Some Indonesian beans are also processed by the semiwashed method.

After processing, the beans are almost fully exposed. The thin parchment covering the beans must be removed, then the beans are polished. Sorting (either by eye or by one of various mechanical methods) and grading (usually determined by size and then by density) are the last steps before storage. The beans are then packed in jute bags that are usually standardized at 130 pounds (60 kilograms). However, new methods skip bagging altogether, and the beans are shipped in huge containers.

If the beans are to be decaffeinated, they are shipped to special factories to do the job. The original methods for decaffeination, which are still in use, involve solvents that are potentially harmful. As an alternative, water-processed or Swiss-processed coffee both involve soaking the beans in water to release and capture the caffeine, and retain more flavor than the solvent methods. (Even though Swiss-processed decaffeination was invented in Switzerland, the only processing plant in the world is in British Columbia.)

ROASTING ⟨

When beans are shipped from their point of origin, they are green and unroasted. Roasting occurs closer to the point of sale—there are many small coffee purveyors and coffeehouses that roast their beans on their premises. Some dedicated coffee lovers roast green beans at home in the oven or in an electric tabletop roaster.

Green coffee beans are very stable and can be stored for a year or so under optimum conditions. These beans have very little taste themselves, and need to be roasted to bring out coffee's characteristic flavors. There are more than two thousand chemical components in green coffee, and they are changed when exposed to heat through a process called "pyrolysis."

Of course, just as with any food, the longer the beans are roasted, the more carbonization occurs. With lighter roasts, more of the inherent flavors of the individual bean type are brought out; in dark-roast coffee, the carbon can take over and mask the coffee's more subtle notes. There is a fashion for dark-roast coffees, but not every bean tastes best roasted to a fare-thee-well. Very dark roasts, with shiny beans and an oily surface roasted to a brittle consistency that grinds easily into a powder, are best reserved for espresso.

There are regional names for the same roasts. This list will be helpful in identifying the roasting terminology that your local coffee purveyor uses.

Light Roast (also cinnamon, half city, light, New England): The beans are roasted to a light brown color similar to cinnamon bark, with a dry surface. This is the roast used for most mass-market commercial brands. The brewed coffee will have light body with no discernible roasted flavor.

Medium (also American, breakfast, medium/high, regular): This is the level that many specialty producers prefer because it allows for more pronounced nuances in the coffee's flavor. The bean still remains dry.

Full Medium (also city, full city, light French, Viennese): A little darker than medium roast; the roasted flavor becomes more pronounced and oil begins to be evident on the surface.

Dark/High Roast (also French, European, New Orleans): The roasting flavor is strong and begins to override the beans' individual taste profile. The beans will be noticeably shiny.

Very Dark Roast (Continental, dark French, heavy, Italian): Shiny, very dark beans with a brittle consistency. The brewed coffee will taste predominantly of the roast.

BREWING THE PERFECT CUP
OF COFFEE ❧

With just a little attention to detail, you can improve your coffee drinking experience. Four major factors affect the final brew: freshness, grind, measurement, and water.

Freshness Just as you wouldn't make a salad with wilted lettuce, the freshness of the beans will affect the brewed coffee. Roasted coffee stales fairly rapidly—most experts say it starts to lose its flavor after one week and is useless after two weeks. When coffee is ground, its essential oils are exposed to the air, which makes ground coffee stale even more quickly. Some people consider ground coffee that is more than three hours old to be stale. For this reason, true coffee lovers buy whole coffee beans and grind them just before using.

Many coffee stores like to sell their beans in big, open barrels, but as exposure to oxygen speeds staling, buy coffee from a purveyor with a brisk turnover, or purchase it in vacuum-packed or valve-fitted bags that keep out the air. When buying coffee online, buy vacuum-packed, as it will stay fresh longer than in regular bags, compensating for shipping time. Do not buy more coffee than you will use within two weeks' time.

Store the coffee in a ceramic or enameled airtight container in a cool, dry place. These containers are preferred over metal and plastic because they don't pick up any flavors and can be washed and dried easily. Contrary to what you may have heard, do not keep coffee in the refrigerator or freezer, as it picks up unwanted moisture and flavors. If you must freeze coffee (say, because you are going away), let it thaw for about 30 minutes before brewing.

Grind The correct grind is essential to making great coffee. Each method of preparation (drip filter, espresso machine, or French press, to name a few) requires a particular grind. If the grind is too fine, the water passes through the coffee too quickly, and the brew is weak. A too coarse grind slows the passage of the water, and the coffee will be strong and bitter. You will find photographs of the correct grind to guide you with the appropriate coffee-making method on pages 19 to 23.

Outside of the old-fashioned box hand grinder, there are essentially two kinds of electric coffee mills for brewing a pot of coffee. A blade grinder chops the beans with a metal propeller. To avoid overheating the beans by the blade's friction, grind the coffee by pressing the on/off button in short bursts.

A burr grinder is preferred by experts, as it makes a more uniform grind. Espresso machines really require a special grinder, since the coffee must be ground to a fineness that is difficult to achieve in anything but the very best burr grinder.

If you like flavored coffees (such as hazelnut or vanilla), grind them in a separate grinder, as the residual aromas and flavors are very hard to remove from the grinder and unflavored beans will pick up the taste.

Measurement The standard recommended ratio of coffee to water is 1½ tablespoons ground coffee to 6 ounces water. This is only good for a point of departure, for, depending on the roast, grind, and other factors, you may have to experiment to find the ratio that you like.

To keep your measurements uniform, use a coffee scoop. Note the volume of the scoop, since scoops can range from one to two tablespoons.

Water Brewed coffee is 97 percent water, so that water had better taste good to begin with. When I was spending a lot of time in Vienna researching my book on Austro-Hungarian desserts, the Viennese coffeehouse owners told me time and again that the real secret of their fine coffee was the water from the nearby mountains.

The water from municipal systems can be too hard, too soft, or too chlorinated to make a good pot of coffee. If your local water has no off flavors, go ahead and use it. Otherwise, filtered (either from a pitcher or an in-line system) or bottled water will make better coffee.

To prepare water for a drip or press coffeemaker, bring the water to a boil, then let it cool for about 15 seconds until the temperature drops to 195° to 205°F. This is the optimum temperature for releasing the flavor compounds in the coffee. Never pour actively boiling water over ground coffee.

THE ESPRESSO EXPERIENCE ❧

There is much more to espresso than dark-roasted coffee. Essentially, espresso is prepared in a special machine that forces hot, pressurized steam through finely ground, dark-roasted coffee beans to extract a small cup of intensely flavored brewed coffee.

Espresso cannot be made carelessly. The beans are dark-roasted to create a slightly sweet, caramelized flavor to balance bitterness, but they should not be black and overroasted. The coffee must be ground just so, then transferred to a metal filter (called a portafilter) and carefully tamped to a density that allows the steam to pass through at a rate that gives the best flavor. The timing of the extraction is important, too. The ideal set by traditional espresso companies (an automatic home machine may differ) is twenty-five seconds to extract one ounce of espresso. The sign of a well-made espresso is a layer of light brown *crema* on its surface.

Expressly Espresso

A demitasse of dark espresso is the springboard for many other beverages.

Americano is named for the American GIs who diluted their espresso with hot water, typically three parts water to one part espresso.

Caffè corretto is an espresso that has been "corrected" with some liquor (such as brandy or grappa), an early morning eye-opener if there ever was one.

Doppio means a "double" of two espresso shots in the same cup.

Caffè latte is espresso combined with hot steamed milk, often with a topping of steamed milk. *Café au lait* is the French version.

Cappuccino gets its name from its topping of steamed milk, which must have reminded an Italian barista of the hood on a Capuchin monk's brown robe. The barista can combine the steamed milk and espresso in an artistic manner to create designs known as latte art.

Espresso con panna is a demitasse of espresso topped with a dollop of freshly whipped cream (not the sweetened aerosol stuff).

Macchiato indicates an espresso "marked" with a dab of steamed milk. A *latte macchiato* is the reverse, with steamed milk marked with a drizzle of espresso.

Mocha (or caffè mocha or mocha latte) is a delicious combination of espresso, hot chocolate, and steamed milk.

Ristretto is "restricted" espresso, as the steam is cut off just before an entire ounce of espresso has been extracted for an especially concentrated shot.

COFFEE POTS AND MACHINES ❧

It wasn't too long ago that the percolator was the premier coffeepot in the American kitchen. Now a plethora of coffee-brewing equipment is available, from a powerful domestic espresso machine to a simple drip filter. I have eliminated some niche coffee brewers (Turkish ibrik, cold-water filter, and vacuum pot) in favor of the most popular methods.

FRENCH PRESS (CAFETIÈRE)

A favorite of European cooks (and, increasingly, upscale American restaurants), the French press makes an especially strong, rich cup of coffee, thanks to a long period of contact between the ground coffee and hot water. A downside is that the coffee cools quickly, so serve it immediately after making or transfer it to a thermos. To keep the grounds from seeping through the filter, use a coarse grind, similar to the texture of kosher salt.

Method

- Rinse the pot and plunger with hot water to warm them.
- Measure the coffee and water into the pot and stir.
- Place the plunger on top of the coffee and water mixture and let steep for four minutes.
- Slowly and firmly press the plunger to force the grounds to the bottom of the pot.

MOKA

This Italian stovetop pot makes very strong coffee similar to espresso. (Authentic espresso requires steam pressure beyond the power of this pot.) Choose your pot according to the amount of servings you usually make, from two to eight servings. The old pots are made from aluminum, which can transfer its flavor to the coffee, but stainless steel pots are now available. Use a fairly fine grind—the ground coffee should be about the same size as sugar crystals.

Method

- Fill the bottom compartment with water up to, but not covering, the safety valve.
- Fill the coffee basket with ground coffee, level with the top of the basket.
- Screw on the top compartment and bring to a boil.
- Remove the pot and serve when the sputtering sound eases.

MANUAL DRIP FILTER

This popular method uses a paper or gold-plated filter, which shortens the length of time that the water is in contact with the coffee. There are choices to be made: Some people believe the brown, unbleached filters transfer less paper flavor to the coffee than the white ones, and others prefer the small amount of sediment that passes through the gold filters to improve the coffee's body. Use a medium grind, about the texture of sand.

Method

- Fit the cone on top of the pot and line with a paper or gold filter (no paper for gold filters).
- Add the coffee to the filter.
- Moisten the coffee with water just off the boil and let it drip through.
- Pour the rest of the water into the filter to complete the brewing.

AUTOMATIC DRIP FILTER

Thanks to its ease of preparation, the electric coffee machine has become ubiquitous. There's a simple trick that will improve your coffee. Clean the pot every month to remove buildup—mix 1 cup distilled white vinegar and 1 cup water and run through the pot, followed by a rinsing cycle of water only. Otherwise, the choice of paper or gold filter is up to you. Use a medium grind.

Method

• Fill the water compartment with cold water.
• Place the paper or gold filter.
• Add the coffee to the filter and place the carafe under the filter.
• Turn the machine on and let brew.

POD COFFEEMAKERS

The ultimate in coffee-making convenience, these coffeemakers use premeasured plastic pods of coffee that come in a large variety of roasts, beans, and flavors. These machines are best for one or two servings. The pods are not interchangeable between brands, so be sure to buy a sufficient supply for your machine, keeping in mind that the pods do have an expiration date.

Method

- Fill the water compartment with cold water.
- Insert the pod into its container.
- Place the cup under the spout.
- Turn the machine on; serve immediately.

ELECTRIC DOMESTIC ESPRESSO MACHINES

These smaller versions of commercial machines bring the espresso bar experience home. Older models are manual—a lever is pulled to push the steam through the coffee grounds. Newer models grind and brew perfect cups with the push of a button. For the best operation, follow the manufacturer's advice on de-scaling the machine to remove mineral buildup. Grind the coffee as finely as superfine sugar.

Method

- Follow the manufacturer's instructions.

HOT AND COLD COFFEE BEVERAGES

Whether you own a top-of-the-line home espresso machine or an automatic drip coffeemaker, there are times when you want to go beyond a basic cup of coffee. Here is a selection of beverages that start with brewed coffee and then take them one (or two) steps further. You'll find coffee drinks from all corners of the world, hot and cold, nonalcoholic and spiked.

❧ SPICED MOCHA

This warm drink is a kind of balancing act, with the caffeinated jolt of espresso enlivening the mellow hot chocolate. It is just the kind of thing you might want to prepare as you settle down with a good book on a wintry afternoon. If you would like to spike it, add a shot of amaretto, rum, or crème de cacao.

1 cup whole milk

One 3-inch cinnamon stick or ¼ teaspoon ground cinnamon

2 tablespoons sugar

1 tablespoon unsweetened cocoa powder

1 tablespoon boiling water

2 ounces hot brewed espresso or Italian- or French-roast coffee prepared in a Moka pot (see page 20)

1. Heat the milk and cinnamon in a small saucepan over low heat until steaming. Remove from the heat and cover. Let stand for 5 minutes. Lift out and discard the cinnamon stick.

2. Stir the sugar and cocoa (and ground cinnamon, if using) together in a large coffee mug. Stir in the boiling water to make a paste. Stir in the hot milk. Return to the saucepan and stir until very hot, but not boiling. Stir in the espresso. Pour back into the mug and serve hot.

CAFÉ BRÛLOT ❧

Makes 4 servings

Flambéed citrus peels and spices give *café brûlot* ("burned coffee" in French) its aromatically smoky citrus flavor. Order it after dinner at a classic New Orleans restaurant such as Antoine's (where it was said to have originated) or Galatoire's, and you will get the full tableside service, with your waiter dramatically ladling streams of flaming liquor into a big silver bowl. At home, you may prefer my streamlined and much safer version, prepared on the stove.

6 whole cloves

1 orange, zest removed in one continuous strip with a vegetable peeler

¼ cup sugar

1 lemon, zest removed in one continuous strip with a vegetable peeler

One 3-inch cinnamon stick, broken in half

½ cup brandy

2 cups hot brewed French-roast coffee, preferably made in a French press (see page 19)

1. Insert the cloves in the orange zest. Combine the sugar, orange and lemon zests, cinnamon, and cloves in a medium saucepan. Pour in the brandy, but do not stir. Heat over low heat until the brandy is warm, about 30 seconds. Carefully ignite the brandy with a long-handled match (be aware that the fumes above the brandy may ignite without the match actually touching the brandy itself). Let burn until the flames burn out by themselves. If the flames haven't extinguished after a minute, cover the saucepan with its lid.

2. Carefully pour the coffee into the saucepan—it will sputter—and stir well to dissolve the sugar. Using tongs, lift out and discard the zests and spices. Ladle the coffee into coffee cups and serve hot.

IRISH COFFEE ❧

Makes 1 serving

When I lived in San Francisco, I spent many a foggy night sipping Irish coffee at the Buena Vista Café, the bar and grill near Fisherman's Wharf that popularized the drink. While there were much more age-appropriate bars for hanging out, my friends and I preferred the BV's Irishes because they were always served piping hot in preheated glasses with a float of thickened fresh cream. Other joints passed off tepid Irishes with—horrors—canned whipped cream spurted on top. Here's how to make a world-class Irish.

Boiling water, to warm the glass	1 sugar cube
¼ cup heavy cream	6 ounces hot brewed medium-roast coffee
1 ounce Irish whisky	

1. Pour boiling water into an Irish coffee glass (a tall, curvy glass mug with a handle) or coffee mug. Let stand for a few minutes to warm the glass.

2. Whisk the cream in a chilled small bowl just until it thickens and takes on some body, but is still pourable. Do not whisk until peaks form.

3. Pour out the hot water and dry the glass. Pour the whisky into the glass, add the sugar cube, and let stand for about 30 seconds to slightly warm the whisky. Pour in the coffee, stirring with a long-handled spoon to dissolve the sugar.

4. Hold the spoon over the coffee with the tip of the spoon touching the surface of the coffee and the rounded back of the spoon facing up. Gently pour the cream over the back of the spoon so it creates a layer floating on the surface of the coffee. Serve at once.

❧ VIENNESE *FIAKER*

Makes 1 serving

When I was writing *Kaffeehaus,* my book on the cafés of Vienna, Budapest, and Prague, I became acquainted with the *Fiaker,* a heady, rum-infused coffee topped with a generous dollop of *Schlagober's* (the Viennese word for whipped cream). Named for the open-topped horse-drawn carriage of the final days of the Hapsburg era (and currently in use to transport tourists around the city), the drink is sure to warm the insides of a chilled carriage driver. Now may be the time to say that cinnamon-flavored Viennese coffee sold at some American coffee purveyors does not exist in Vienna itself, and that real Viennese coffee is medium-roast and drip-brewed.

Boiling water, to warm the mug

3 tablespoons golden rum

1 teaspoon superfine or granulated sugar

1 cup hot brewed medium-roast coffee

Whipped Cream (page 120)

1. Fill a coffee mug with boiling water and let stand for 1 minute to warm the mug. Pour out the water and dry the mug.

2. Pour the rum into the cup and stir in the sugar. Add the coffee. Top with the whipped cream. Serve hot.

VIETNAMESE COFFEE

Vietnamese coffee is all about ritual and patience. A special metal coffee filter, which looks very much like a small top hat, is filled with coffee, topped with a damper, and placed over the cup. Boiling water is added, and it drips very slowly through the filter to make a dark, deeply flavored brew. For the most authentic flavor, use coffee flavored with chicory, an additive that the Vietnamese learned to appreciate during the French occupation, which is very similar to New Orleans–style chicory-flavored coffee. Be sure that the beans aren't finely ground or the coffee will drip too quickly and you won't get the right depth of flavor. Buy Vietnamese coffee filters at Asian markets and online at www.amazon.com or www.importfoods.com.

1 heaping tablespoon medium-grind French-roast coffee or coffee with chicory

¾ cup boiling water

1 to 2 tablespoons sweetened condensed milk, as needed

Sugar, as needed

1. A Vietnamese coffee filter has three parts: the filter with a perforated bottom, a perforated damper, and a lid that doubles as a saucer to hold the filter after brewing. Remove the damper and place the coffee in the filter. Tap the filter on the counter to settle the coffee. Return the damper to the filter and screw it in to compress the coffee. (Some dampers do not screw in place, and should be placed on top of the coffee and used to lightly tamp the coffee.) Place the filter over the cup.

2. Add about 2 tablespoons of the boiling water to the filter, just enough to cover the coffee. Let drip for about 30 seconds. Unscrew the damper a turn or two. Slowly pour the remaining water into the filter and cover the filter with the lid. Wait until the water has completely dripped through the filter, about 5 minutes. Place the lid on the table, then lift up and remove the filter and place it on the lid.

3. Add condensed milk to taste and sugar to taste, and stir. Serve at once.

ICED VIETNAMESE COFFEE Pour the brewed coffee over ice into a tall glass. (Cool the coffee, if you wish.) Add sweetened condensed milk and sugar syrup (see page 35) to taste.

COFFEE FRAPPE

What the rest of the country calls a milkshake, New Englanders call a frappe. (Note that it is not a *frappé*, the French term for a frothy drink, and the Greek name for their favorite iced coffee made with sweet instant coffee shaken until foamy and served with a float of evaporated milk.) Frappes are often made with coffee syrup, but you can get an even more refined flavor with espresso or Moka-brewed Italian roast coffee. Add sugar to the blender and sweeten to taste, if you wish, but this recipe is sweet enough for me.

4 scoops (about 1½ cups) vanilla ice cream

¼ cup brewed espresso or Italian-roast coffee
prepared in a Moka pot (see page 20), cold

½ cup whole milk, as needed

Combine the ice cream and espresso in a blender. Turn the machine on and add enough milk to give the drink the desired thickness. Divide the frappe equally into two tall glasses and serve immediately.

MOCHA FRAPPE Pour 1 tablespoon chocolate syrup into each glass. Use a long-handled spoon to smear the syrup up the sides of each glass. Pour in the coffee frappe and serve immediately.

❧ THAI ICED COFFEE

When American military bases were established in Thailand, sweetened condensed milk was sold at the commissaries. It didn't take long for the Thais to use it to lighten and sweeten their coffee. In the States, some people add cardamom or cinnamon to make a kind of coffee chai. The spices are added to simulate the flavor of authentic Thai coffee (spelled *oliang* or *oleang*, dark-roast coffee augmented with soybeans, corn, or chicory), which is made with a muslin filter (used for either tea or coffee) that resembles a small, long butterfly net. Although you can buy both the Thai tea filter coffee and the authentic coffee at www.amazon.com, this version is simplified to use handy ingredients and implements. As the coffee is strong to begin with, don't worry about the ice cubes melting and diluting the drink.

2 cups hot brewed French-roast coffee, preferably made in a French press (see page 19)

½ teaspoon ground cardamom

Ice cubes

About ½ cup sweetened condensed milk, as needed

Pinch of ground cinnamon (optional)

Sugar syrup (optional, see opposite)

1. Combine the coffee and cardamom. Fill two tall glasses with ice cubes.

2. Divide the coffee equally between the glasses. Top each with condensed milk to taste. Garnish with a sprinkle of ground cinnamon, if desired. Serve at once, with long spoons to stir the milk into the coffee. If you would like sweeter coffee, add the syrup to taste.

Sugar Syrup

Makes about ¾ cup

Granulated sugar will stubbornly refuse to dissolve in iced drinks. Superfine sugar (also called bartenders' sugar) will readily dissipate, but it isn't a standard kitchen item. The solution—no pun intended—is sugar syrup, which is easy to prepare and can be stored for a month or two in the refrigerator. This also goes by the names "simple syrup" and "bar syrup."

½ cup granulated sugar

1. Bring the sugar and ½ cup water to a boil in a small saucepan over high heat, stirring to dissolve the sugar. When the syrup is boiling, stop stirring and reduce the heat to medium. Cook for 1 minute. Remove from the heat and let cool.

2. Pour into a glass jar and cover. Refrigerate until ready to use. (The syrup can be refrigerated for up to 2 months.) Use as a sweetener in cold or hot drinks.

❧ CARAMEL FREEZE

Makes 2 servings

This slush is one of the best reasons I know for having iced coffee cubes in the freezer. It is miles better than any expensive frozen concoction that you could buy at your local café. If you want to top it with a big dollop of whipped cream, go ahead.

½ cup store-bought caramel sauce or ice cream topping, as needed

12 iced coffee cubes, made from about 1½ cups frozen coffee (see opposite)

½ cup whole milk

1. Pour about 1½ tablespoons of the caramel sauce into a tall glass. Use a long-handled spoon to smear it up the sides of the glass. Repeat with a second glass.

2. Combine the remaining sauce, the iced coffee cubes, and the milk in a blender. Process until the mixture is smooth. Divide evenly between the glasses and serve immediately.

Iced Coffee Cubes

In the warm days of summer, I find there's no better afternoon pick-me-up than a frosty glass of iced coffee. Lovers of iced tea may argue, but tea, as good as it is, simply doesn't have enough caffeine to revive flagging spirits in quite the same way.

The problem with iced coffee is that regular ice cubes water it down, and what begins as a bracing beverage can quickly dilute into a watery sludge. Substitute cubes of frozen coffee for the ice cubes, and the problem disappears.

Here's how to make iced coffee cubes. Don't toss out the leftover coffee from the morning pot. Instead, let the coffee cool. Pour the coffee into an ice cube tray and freeze. (Figure on about 2 tablespoons of coffee per cube.) When the cubes are solid, pop them out of the tray into a zippered plastic storage bag and freeze until needed, up to two months.

In a perfect world, the best iced coffee is made with cold brewed coffee. When you don't have the time to let the coffee cool, just pour hot brewed coffee over frozen coffee cubes for a quick iced coffee. The cubes will melt, but at least the coffee won't get watered down.

As a bonus, frozen coffee cubes can be blended with other ingredients to make wonderful at-home versions of the pricey coffee slushes sold at cafés. See Caramel Freeze (opposite) for the basic recipe and let your imagination go from there.

❧ ESPRESSO MARTINI

Caffeinated cocktails appear on the menus of many hip lounges from Los Angeles to New York, perhaps ensuring that drinkers will be able to stay awake to the wee hours of the morning. When I serve this libation to people who are neither espresso nor martini fans, they immediately change their tune and swear their allegiance to both beverages. Use vodka with a neutral taste, such as Absolut or Smirnoff. If you think about it, pop the vodka and crème de cacao into the freezer for an hour or two before making the drink so the liquors are very cold.

Ice cubes

2 ounces brewed espresso or French- or Italian-roast coffee prepared in a drip pot (see page 22) or a Moka pot (see page 20), chilled

2 ounces vodka, preferably chilled

1 ounce clear crème de cacao, preferably chilled

Heavy cream, as needed

1. Chill a martini glass in the freezer for 5 minutes.

2. Fill a cocktail shaker with ice cubes. Add the coffee, vodka, and crème de cacao and shake well. Pour into the glass.

3. Hold a dessert spoon over the martini with the tip of the spoon touching the surface and the rounded back of the spoon facing up. Gently pour the cream over the back of the spoon so it creates a layer floating on the surface of the martini. Serve at once.

CAFFÈ AFFOGATO

Makes 1 serving

Simple but elegant, caffè affogato is a scoop or two of gelato or ice cream with espresso poured over the top. Is it a drink or a dessert? That depends on whether you eat the gelato with a spoon while it is still semifrozen or you let it melt to flavor the coffee. I make this often for the easiest of after-dinner treats, as it combines dessert with a postprandial beverage. A piping-hot shot of authentic espresso (that is, from an electric machine) is traditional, but I find it melts the gelato too quickly when making more than one serving. My preference is to brew the coffee in a Moka pot, then let it cool to tepid before serving, then pour the coffee over the gelato at the table so it can be served immediately.

2 scoops vanilla gelato or ice cream (see Note)

2 ounces brewed espresso or Italian- or French-roast coffee prepared in a Moka pot (see page 20), cooled to tepid

Put the gelato in a heatproof glass or bowl. Pour the coffee over the gelato and serve immediately.

NOTE: Vanilla and coffee are old friends, but other flavors of gelato work well, too. Try chocolate or dulce de leche.

A CAKE PRIMER

$\mathcal{B}$efore baking a cake, it helps to have some guidelines on the basic ingredients, equipment, and techniques that you will use again and again. Even if you are an experienced baker, take some time to read this material as a refresher course.

INGREDIENTS

Cakes, like all baking, are a balance of ingredients. But even more than other pastries, with cakes, the balance is quite delicate. For example, switching one flour for another can give entirely different results. Here is a glossary of common baking ingredients, and suggestions for their use when making cakes.

FLOUR

Flour is the backbone of all cake recipes. Milled from wheat, flour is mostly starch, but also contains proteins. These proteins give structure to baked goods—without them, the cake would collapse. When two of these proteins, gliadin and glutenin, are moistened with water and mixed, they form gluten, an invisible system in the dough. The more the dough is manipulated, the stronger the gluten structure becomes.

Bread dough is kneaded to create a strong gluten structure for chewy, crusty bread. When it comes to cake, the batter should be mixed just long enough to incorporate the flour to keep gluten formation at a minimum to create tender cakes. (In some cases, as with génoise, the flour is only folded in, and not stirred at all.)

Professionals designate flour as hard or soft, depending on the amount of potential gluten in the flour. Bread bakers prefer hard flour because their dough must have a strong gluten structure that can withstand kneading, and give a finished result with a crisp crust and chewy texture. Bread and unbleached flour are considered hard flours.

All-purpose flour is a combination of hard and soft flours. *Bleached all-purpose flour* has been chemically treated to lengthen its shelf life, and the bleaching process also reduces the protein, making for tender cakes. *Unbleached all-purpose flour* has had the hull and bran removed before milling, and it has a relatively high protein content that some bakers find gives their cakes a firmer crumb.

As tenderness is a major criterion for cakes, you will get the most delicate from bleached all-purpose flour. Some bakers prefer unbleached flour because it hasn't been chemically treated, and they feel that it has better flavor. In recipes with a high proportion of butter and sugar (both of which are tenderizers), you can substitute unbleached for bleached flour, if you prefer, but expect the baked cake to have a slightly tougher texture. You may not even notice it unless you do a side-by-side comparison. So, the choice between bleached and unbleached flour is yours.

Pastry chefs often use softer flours to give a cake a desirable tender crumb. *Cake flour* is soft flour that has been bleached and finely milled. For example, angel food cake has no fat to act as a tenderizer, so it is made with cake flour to guard against toughness. As with bleached all-purpose flour, some bakers avoid cake flour because it is highly processed. However, King Arthur now sells unbleached cake flour, and it is worth searching out large natural-food supermarkets. If you wish, for each cup of cake flour, substitute 1 cup (minus 1 tablespoon) all-purpose flour sifted with 1 tablespoon cornstarch. The cornstarch, which has no gluten, will effectively lower the protein content of the flour. When buying cake flour, look carefully at the label and avoid "self-rising" flours, as they include leavenings as a so-called convenience to the baker. It is better to add the necessary leavenings yourself to carefully control the rise. The flour in this book was measured by the dip-and-sweep method (see page 51).

BUTTER

There is no substitute for the creamy flavor of butter, and it also is an important building block in cake batter. Mixing aerates the butter to create air bubbles that are part of the leavening process.

Butter is available unsalted or salted. Unsalted butter is best because the baker is in control over how much salt will be added to the recipe. Salt was originally added to butter to cover up any off flavors and to lengthen its shelf life, neither of which are especially positive improvements.

When the butter will be creamed, the recipe's ingredient list instructs to have the butter "at room temperature." This is a useful phrase, but not entirely accurate, unless your kitchen is exactly 68°F, which is the optimum temperature for beating air into the butter during the creaming process. The butter should stand at room temperature until it has a malleable, almost plastic consistency, with a dull, not shiny, appearance. In general, this takes about 30 minutes for a stick of butter. One of the most common baking mistakes occurs when the butter for creaming is too soft, reducing the number of bubbles created and resulting in an underrisen cake.

If you don't have the time to let the cold butter stand at room temperature and soften on its own, there are options. Cut the butter into ½-inch cubes and let stand in a warm spot in the kitchen for about 15 minutes (use this time to preheat the oven, assemble the ingredients, and prepare the pan). Or grate the chilled butter on the large holes of a box grater into the mixing bowl. Do not use a microwave, as it is too easy to melt and not soften the butter.

Some recipes call for melted butter. To give the butter deeper flavor, I often let it cook until it is browned. Melt the butter in a small, heavy-bottomed saucepan over medium-low heat, and bring to a boil. Let the butter boil for a minute or so until the milk solids in the bottom of the pan turn a light nutty brown, about the color of walnut shells. Remove from the heat and let stand 1 minute. Using a soup spoon, skim the foam from the surface of the melted butter. Pour the clear yellow melted butter into a bowl, leaving the browned milk solids in the saucepan. The melted butter must be cooled to tepid before using.

EGGS

Eggs moisten the cake batter, also giving it an elasticity that traps air and contributes to rising. The eggs should be at room temperature, which makes them easier to be absorbed into the dough. The discrepancy in temperature between creamed butter and sugar and chilled eggs can make a batter curdle. And room-temperature eggs have the best elasticity and ability to expand when beaten.

To quickly bring cold eggs to room temperature, place the uncracked eggs in a bowl, cover with hot tap water, and let stand for about 5 minutes. Eggs are easier to separate when they are chilled. For separated eggs, place the yolks or whites in separate bowls, place each bowl in a larger bowl of warm water, and let stand until the contents lose their chill, about 5 minutes.

SUGAR

Classic cakes use sugar as the main sweetener. Sugar can be processed from either sugarcane or sugar beets. Most bakers prefer cane sugar, as beet sugar doesn't behave reliably in all applications (such as melting to make caramel). Look for "cane sugar" on the packaging. *Granulated sugar*, with medium-size crystals, is the sugar most often used for cake batters.

Confectioners' sugar, also called "powdered sugar," is finely ground sugar with a little cornstarch added to discourage clumping. It is used for icings and frostings and for decorating, and is usually sifted before using to remove lumps. The term "6x" on confectioners' sugar packaging means that the sugar was sifted six times to ensure a powdery texture.

Superfine sugar, also known as bartenders' or bar sugar, is finely granulated to dissolve readily in icings, meringues, and beverages. If you wish, you can make it by processing an equal amount of granulated sugar in a food processor for a few minutes, or until very finely ground.

Brown sugar used to be a by-product of the sugar-making process, but these days it is usually just crystallized sugar that has been sprayed with molasses for flavor and color. The amount of molasses creates light or dark sugar, which are interchangeable, depending on how much molasses flavor you like. *Muscovado sugar* is brown sugar made by a traditional method, a factor that adds to its cost. It has a deeper flavor than standard brown sugar, and, while pricey, does boost the flavor of baked goods. Always store brown sugar in an airtight container to retain its moisture and keep it from drying into lumps. Don't use lumpy brown sugar in a cake batter, as it will not dissolve and the cake will have large holes in the crumb. To return lumpy brown sugar to its original state, rub it through a coarse-mesh wire sieve to break down the lumps.

LEAVENING

The two most common leavenings for cakes are baking powder and baking soda. (A third possible leavening, yeast, is not used in this book.) Some cakes, such as angel food and génoise, are leavened only by the air beaten into the eggs and do not use chemical leavenings, which work on the chemical reaction that occurs when an acid and an alkali are mixed. During mixing, tiny air bubbles are incorporated into the cake batter. The leavenings create carbon dioxide to inflate the bubbles, making the cake rise. Look closely at a piece of cake, and you can see the web of bubbles connected by strands of batter.

Baking soda (bicarbonate of soda) is an alkali. Mix it with an acidic ingredient (such as buttermilk, sour cream, vinegar, lemon juice, brown sugar, molasses, or natural cocoa powder), moisten it, and carbon dioxide forms. If the acidic ingredient is not present in the recipe, the baking soda can't do its work, and the cake will be flat with a soapy taste.

Baking powder does not need an acidic ingredient to be activated. It is made of baking soda combined with a dry acidic ingredient (usually aluminum sodium sulfate). When moistened, the baking powder creates carbon dioxide to make the cake rise. Commercial baking powder is almost always labeled "double-acting," which means that the baking powder is initially activated when moistened, with a second burst of leavening the batter occurring from the heat of the oven. Some bakers, myself included, find that baking powders with aluminum by-products have a bitter flavor that can be detected. I recommend Rumford's, which does not contain aluminum.

There are recipes that use both baking soda and baking powder. The soda acts to neutralize the acid ingredients, providing a small amount of the leavening in the process, while the baking powder does the bulk of the work.

MILK

All ingredients for cake batter should be at room temperature for the most efficient mixing. Milk is no exception. Let the measured milk stand at room temperature for about an hour so it loses its chill, or place the measuring cup in a bowl of hot water for a few minutes. Or microwave it in a microwave-safe container on low (20% power) in 10-second periods, stirring after each increment, until it is tepid. Do not let buttermilk come to a boil or it could curdle.

Whole milk, which contains fat, will give your cake the most tender crumb. If you substitute reduced-, low-, or nonfat milk, you are also reducing the amount of fat, and the cake could come out tough.

The acids that provide *buttermilk* with its tanginess are also effective tenderizers, giving cakes a melt-in-your-mouth texture. It may surprise you to know that most commercial buttermilk has a low-butterfat content—very few dairies make full-fat buttermilk. Serious cake bakers always have buttermilk in the refrigerator ready to put into action. It keeps for a couple of weeks after opening. Dried buttermilk, which is reconstituted with water, has a much thinner texture than the real thing, and is not recommended. If you need to make a substitute, for every cup of buttermilk, whisk ⅔ cup low-fat yogurt with ⅓ cup whole milk. Buttermilk separates during storage, so shake the carton well before using.

SALT

Without a little salt in the batter, cakes can taste flat. This is especially true of chocolate cakes. In cakes, salt is used sparingly as a flavor enhancer and is not a prominent taste itself, so the most important factor is how easily the salt dissolves. (This isn't the case in savory cooking, where coarse salt can be purposely used to add texture to a dish.) Fine sea salt, which also has a clean, neutral flavor, is my first choice, but plain table salt will also work well. Kosher salt is too coarse and its large crystals may not pass through the sieve when sifted. If you only have coarse salt in your kitchen, grind it first in a spice grinder or mortar and pestle before using in baking.

CHOCOLATE AND COCOA

One of the world's most beloved flavors, for all its ubiquity, chocolate is a fairly complex subject. *Unsweetened chocolate* is cacao beans that have been roasted, ground, molded, and cooled. Professionals sometimes call it "chocolate liquor." It contains no sugar.

Semisweet or bittersweet chocolate contains chocolate liquor that has been sweetened to some degree. The USDA doesn't have a specific standard for semisweet or bittersweet chocolate, and only has a category "dark chocolate," which means any chocolate with a minimum of 35 percent cacao. This is fairly meaningless because no producers make chocolate with such low cacao content. The average cacao content in semisweet chocolate is around 55 percent, with the remaining contents being sugar, the emulsifier lecithin, and vanilla (or vanillin). However, one brand's semisweet can be another's bittersweet. Many chocolate brands now state the cacao percentage on the label. If it isn't listed, you can assume that it isn't above 62 percent. I

use Callebaut semisweet chocolate, which is easily found in bulk at many natural food stores and supermarkets, for my "house chocolate." Trader Joe's also has an excellent brand of Belgian bulk chocolate.

High-percentage chocolate has a larger proportion of cacao, which naturally gives it a richer chocolate flavor. If you like a bitter note to your eating chocolate, you will like high-percentage chocolate, but it can make for trouble in baking. The higher cacao content can wreak havoc with a recipe, as the proportions of sugar and other ingredients (such as the fat supplied by cocoa butter in the chocolate) are thrown off. For this reason, to guarantee good results in certain recipes, I recommend chocolate with a cacao content of no higher than 62 percent.

Milk chocolate is sweeter than semisweet chocolate and has been flavored with dried milk solids. While not used in this book, you might find it useful to know that *white chocolate* contains no cacao at all, and that the best brands are basically sweetened cocoa butter flavored with vanilla. Both of these chocolates are delicate and can scorch easily, so melt them with an extra measure of caution.

Chocolate chips are processed with an additional amount of lecithin to keep them from melting too quickly in the oven.

Chocolate has two enemies, heat and water. When melting, care should be taken to avoid overheating, and the chocolate should not come into contact with water (or even steam). The traditional way to melt chocolate is in a double boiler set over hot water, and it is a good method.

Chop the chocolate into small pieces with a serrated knife. (The serrated knife grips the chocolate better than a straight-edge one, and you have less chance of cutting yourself. Do not chop chocolate in a food processor, as the friction can heat and melt the chocolate.) And while it may be tempting to use chocolate chips to skip the chore of chopping the chocolate, the extra lecithin in the chips makes them difficult to melt. If you bake a lot and want to save time from chopping, look for *chocolate callets*, small disks of chocolate made expressly for melting.

Put the chopped chocolate in the top part of a double-boiler or a heatproof bowl. Bring a couple of inches of water to a boil in the bottom part of the double boiler or a medium saucepan. Remove the pan from the heat. Place the double-boiler insert or a metal or glass bowl over the water and let stand, stirring occasionally, until the chocolate is smooth and melted.

An alternative to the double-boiler method uses a skillet. This method is excellent because it lets the bowl (and therefore the chocolate) come into contact with a larger heating surface, and reduces the melting time. Fill a skillet with about ½ inch of water and bring it to a simmer over medium heat. Reduce the heat to very low so the water is barely bubbling. Place the chopped chocolate in a heatproof bowl with a wide bottom. Carefully place the bowl in the hot water, taking care not to let any water splash into the chocolate. Let stand, stirring occasionally, until smooth and melted.

The microwave provides another method for melting chocolate. Put the chocolate in a microwave-safe bowl. Microwave the chocolate on medium (50%) power in 30-second increments, stirring well after each period, until the chocolate is smooth and melted. The chocolate may not look melted until it is stirred.

Cocoa powder is pulverized, unsweetened cacao beans. *Natural cocoa powder,* such as the familiar Hershey's in the brown box, is the cocoa that Americans always baked with in the past because nothing else was readily available. It is acidic, and recipes that use it usually call for baking soda to neutralize it. *Dutch-processed cocoa* has been treated with alkali to reduce its acidity and deepen its color (the procedure was invented in the Netherlands in the 1830s). If a cake calls for Dutch-processed cocoa, it can be leavened with baking powder, as the acidity of the cocoa has been reduced so much that baking soda isn't needed to neutralize it.

Always use the cocoa called for in the recipe. When I am developing recipes with cocoa, I usually opt for natural cocoa for a traditional American flavor and Dutch-processed cocoa for a darker color with a slightly milder chocolate impact. (And any cake with natural cocoa and baking soda will acquire a naturally dark color anyway, thanks to the chemical reaction between the two.) I have used natural cocoa powder in most of the recipes in this book. In the cases where there is a choice between the two cocoas, I have indicated Dutch-processed cocoa as my first choice because of its dark color for aesthetic reasons, but natural cocoa will work, too. For beverages, use either cocoa.

VANILLA

If you have ever wondered why vanilla is relatively expensive, consider this: The vanilla orchid, which only grows in tropical regions, must be hand-pollinated for commercial use, and the flower only opens one day a year. The good news for bakers is that vanilla is used in small amounts, so your investment lasts a long time.

Vanilla beans and their seeds are often used to flavor custards, ice creams, sweet fillings, and desserts or their components, but the beans' delicate aroma and flavor can be lost in batters unless the baker uses an inordinate amount. Vanilla extract is the more effective and common way to infuse vanilla flavor into baked goods. Imitation vanilla extract (vanillin) is a by-product of paper manufacturing, reason enough not to use it. However, more than one taste panel has determined that there is little flavor difference between real and artificial vanilla. So, while I prefer to stick with the real thing, the choice is yours.

High-quality vanilla extract often has its beans' source on the label. Madagascar-Bourbon indicates that the beans come from two of the most highly regarded locations for vanilla plantations (Bourbon is the former name of the island of Réunion). Mexican vanilla is very similar in flavor. Tahitian vanilla has a distinctive, perfumed aroma. Again, although I like the full rounded flavor of Madagascar-Bourbon, there is room for personal preference.

FOOD COLORING

Food coloring adds vibrant hues to icings and frostings, but there are other uses—without it, Red Velvet Cupcakes would merely be Brown Velvet Cupcakes. Food coloring comes in three forms: liquid, paste, and gel. Gel, which gives the richest colors, is my favorite. Just stir it, drop by drop, into the food, but gauge the color carefully, as it is so concentrated that it is easy to go overboard and tint *too* saturated. My favorite brand is Spectrum, made by Ateco, as its colors are deep and very attractive. You can find individual hues or a six- or twelve-pack of the most popular colors in small plastic bottles at cake decorating suppliers and hobby shops. Food colorings with all-natural ingredients are available at natural food grocery stores, but you may find the colors to be muted.

Measuring

Bakers love to argue about measuring ingredients, especially when it comes to flour, as its fluffy texture makes it especially susceptible to variations in measurement methods. Professional bakers always weigh their ingredients, while most home bakers prefer measuring cups. After interviewing many of my baking students in my classes around the country, I know that the vast majority of home bakers don't own an electric scale, and that they are going to use volume measurements anyway. Therefore, I provide only volume measurements here.

That being said, there is another problem with volume measuring that must be addressed. Some bakers spoon the flour into a measuring cup, and others simply dip the cup into the flour's container to fill the cup. Each method gives a different weight. The flour in this book has been measured by the dip-and-sweep method. Dip a dry-ingredient (metal or plastic) cup into the flour to fill it. Take care that there are no air pockets in the cup, but don't pack the flour. Sweep away the excess flour with the edge of a knife so the flour remaining in the cup is level with the cup's edge.

EQUIPMENT ✦

OVENS

Take it from me—ovens are notoriously unreliable. In the last five years, I have had three brand-name ovens in my kitchen, and only one heated to a temperature within a reasonable range of the number set on the thermostat.

To keep the cake a safe distance from the heat source and avoid overbrowning, position the oven rack in the center of the oven. Preheat the oven thoroughly before putting in the cake pans. In most ovens, this takes 15 to 20 minutes, which is a fine time to gather the ingredients for the recipe.

For accuracy's sake, always test the oven temperature with an *oven thermometer.* The best thermometers have alcohol-filled glass gauges, but spring-operated thermometers with dial faces can be good, too. The most important factor is the visibility of the numbers. Place the thermometer where the cake will be baked—in the center of the oven rack, well away from the sides.

Many ovens have the option for convection baking, but most of the home cooks I know are simply afraid of it. Convection baking uses a fan to circulate the hot air in the oven, which promotes browning and cooks food more quickly. When using convection baking, decrease the standard temperature in a recipe by 25°F, and estimate that the cakes will bake in about two-thirds of the estimated baking time. You will have to rely on visual and touch tests to check for doneness, but that's a good idea for any kind of cooking, whether convection is used or not. Frankly, I suspect that the blowing air (which could be stronger in some ovens than others) may be detrimental to delicate, egg-based cakes without chemical leaveners, such as angel food and génoise, so I advise against convection baking for those recipes.

ELECTRIC MIXERS

A *heavy-duty standing electric mixer* has become standard in the passionate home baker's kitchen. Cake bakers will use the paddle blade attachment for creaming butter and sugar and subsequent batter mixing, and the whisk attachment for whipping eggs and cream. (The dough hook is reserved for kneading bread dough in the work bowl.) The 5-quart model is the most versatile size. The smaller 4½-quart mixer is too small for some batters and icings, and the larger models are too spacious to mix single batches of most recipes. A second bowl for your mixer is a great time-saver if you want to move ahead to mixing a frosting without having to stop and wash the first bowl.

Even if you have a standing mixer, an *electric hand mixer* is also useful when whipping small amounts of cream or egg whites. The whisk attachment on a standing mixer just won't reach deep enough into the bowl to whip any less than four egg whites or one cup of heavy cream. Of course, you can always whisk these small amounts by hand, but a hand mixer does these jobs in a jiffy. A standing mixer is not necessary for the recipes in this book; a hand mixer will work, too. However, when beating large amounts of eggs or whites with a hand mixer, such as those required by génoise or angel food cake, be sure to set the mixer on high and to allow enough time for the eggs to beat to the optimum volume.

BAKING PANS

The best pans for baking are made from heavy-gauge, high-quality aluminum. They are sturdy and absorb oven heat evenly. Nonstick pans may seem like a good idea, but their dark color retains heat, and it is easy to overcook food baked in them. (The dark black steel pans are especially notorious for this drawback.) If you must use them, reduce the oven temperature by 25°F and watch the food carefully to avoid burning. Oblong baking pans are often made from Pyrex. As this tempered glass also retains heat, cakes baked in it should also be baked 25°F lower than the recipe states. Here are the various cake pans used in this book:

Round cake pans come in a variety of sizes, but the 8- and 9-inch round pans with 1½-inch sides are the most versatile for the home baker who isn't baking a wedding cake! To remove the baked cakes easily from the pans, line the bottoms with parchment or wax paper rounds before adding the batter (see page 56).

Oblong and square pans are good sizes for coffee cakes that provide a moderate number of servings. I use 11½ x 8-inch oblong and 8-inch square pans in this book. It is interesting to note that an 8-inch round pan holds 25 percent less than a square pan, so keep that in mind if you feel like changing pans for a different look.

Loaf pans come in three standard sizes: 9 x 5, 8½ x 4½, and 8 x 4 inches. I use the first pan. At a glance, it may seem that there isn't much difference in the pan capacities, but actually the pans listed hold, respectively, 8, 6, and 4 cups.

Springform pans are tall pans with removable sides. Most are made in Europe, so their dimensions are really measured in the metric system. Therefore, a 9-inch round springform pan may truly be 24 centimeters, or closer to 9½ inches. Luckily, this is a minor discrepancy, so don't let it drive you crazy. It is worth buying a high-quality pan, even if the price is higher than the standard version, because the clips holding the sides are stronger and the pan will last longer. A springform pan is usually put into action for baking a cheesecake, but it is also the perfect pan for making a tall génoise cake that will be sliced into layers.

Muffin pans are the pans of choice for cupcakes. The average muffin cup measures 2¾ inches in diameter and 1¼ inches high, with a capacity of about 7 tablespoons, and this is the size used for the cupcake recipes in this book. There are "standard" muffin pans with slightly larger or smaller capacities (not to mention "jumbo" and miniature muffin pans), and using them will throw off the recipe yield.

Fluted tube pans are commonly called Bundt pans. (*Bund* means group in German. The pans were originally designed for members of the German-American community who wanted an American-made equivalent to the European *kugelhupf* pans, which were difficult to import after World War II.) These pans are now made in a variety of imaginative designs beyond the familiar "turban" shape. If the pan is nonstick and dark colored, start testing the cake for doneness about 10 minutes earlier than the recipe states to avoid overbaking.

A *tube pan with a removable bottom* is essential for angel food and chiffon cakes. Do not use a nonstick tube pan, as these batters need a tactile surface to give them traction when rising. Both cakes are cooled upside down, so look for a pan with raised feet around the top edge to lift the cake above the counter.

UTENSILS AND TOOLS

A *coarse-mesh wire sieve* does a great job of sifting dry ingredients. Do not use a fine-mesh sieve, which should be reserved for straining the tiny seeds from raspberry puree and the like.

Rubber (or silicone) spatulas are used to scrape ingredients down from the sides of a bowl during mixing, or to transfer every bit of batter from the bowl to the cake pan. Silicone spatulas are heat-resistant (some up to 800°F), so they are perfect for cooking and stirring hot ingredients on the stove, especially sticky ones that need to be occasionally scraped from the sides of the saucepan.

A *large offset metal spatula* is the tool for spreading batter evenly in the pan. Use a *small offset spatula* for frosting cupcakes.

You will find a *large balloon whisk,* at least 12 inches long and 6 inches wide at the bulbous part of the whisk, to be the best tool for folding flour into the egg foam in sponge cakes.

A long 12- to 14-inch *serrated knife* is best for cutting a whole cake into layers.

A bristle *pastry brush* will help apply the sugar syrup that flavors sponge cakes. A silicone brush doesn't work as well, as it doesn't soak up the syrup.

Use a high-quality *ice cream scoop* with about ½-cup capacity to transfer cupcake batter easily from the bowl to the muffin cups.

Wire cake racks raise cakes above the counter so that they can cool more quickly. You'll need at least two racks to help flip cakes right side up after unmolding. Large rectangular racks can easily hold a large batch of cupcakes or two cake layers, but round racks to hold a single cake are easier to use when flipping layers. You may want to have both kinds.

Bakers love *parchment paper* for its nonstick and heat-resistant properties. In cake baking, it is most often used to line a cake pan to keep the batter from adhering to the bottom. (Its other main kitchen job is to cover baking sheets when baking cookies.) You can use wax paper for lining pans because it will be covered and protected by batter, but do not use it for lining baking sheets, as it will be exposed and burn in the oven. Parchment paper commonly comes in rolls, but it is very difficult to uncurl. With a little searching online, you can find flat sheets of parchment paper cut to fit half-sheet pans, which eliminates the curling problem. Boxed sheets of parchment paper cut to fit full-sheet pans are sold at restaurant suppliers. I shared the expense of a box with other home bakers, and we now all have (close to) lifetime supplies. (The large sheets need to be cut in half to fit the common half-sheet, which is a fair trade-off for the convenience of flat parchment paper.)

If you bake a lot of layer cakes, you may want to buy precut parchment paper rounds. The 9-inch diameter is a versatile size, as it can be trimmed to fit an 8-inch pan or used to line 9- or 10-inch pans (don't worry about the small amount of exposed bottom in the larger pan).

Cardboard cake rounds make sturdy bases to hold cakes. Trim the round about ½ inch smaller than the cake layer so it isn't visible, or buy cake rounds an inch smaller than your standard cake. For example, use an 8-inch round for a 9-inch cake.

To give your frosted cake a professional finish, use a pastry bag and tips. The two brands that you will see most often at cake decorating suppliers and hobby shops are Ateco and Wilton. Buy a *large pastry bag* at least 12 inches long, as smaller bags don't hold enough frosting. *Pastry tips* are identified by numbers. You don't need a large collection of tips. For decorating cakes with simple rosettes and swirls, a ½-inch diameter star tip, such as Ateco #825, is sufficient. For a similar but more articulated look, use a French star tip of the same size, such as Ateco #865, but the two are really interchangeable. To make the flower petals for the Classic Yellow Cupcakes with Big Buttercream Flowers on page 95, use Wilton #81, which is a smaller tip that requires a plastic coupler to fit the pastry bag.

TECHNIQUES ❧

There are two basic kinds of cake, butter cake and sponge cake. *Butter cakes* start by creaming butter and sugar together, with additions of eggs, flour, and flavorings. They are usually leavened with baking powder or baking soda, and are the tender cakes used for many American-style layer cakes. *Sponge cakes* have a more resilient texture, and start with eggs and sugar beaten into foam, with flour carefully folded in. The air beaten into the eggs supplies most of the leavening power to these cakes, which may or may not include chemical leavenings, too. Génoise and angel food are examples of sponge cakes.

PREPARATIONS

Position the rack in the center of the oven, then thoroughly preheat the oven. The correct temperature is important to start the leavening, expand the air bubbles, and set the batter.

Be sure that all the ingredients are at room temperature. If necessary, warm the eggs or milk in a bowl of hot water, and soften the butter to the proper malleable consistency.

Butter and flour the cake pan(s) as directed. (For angel food cake, leave the pan ungreased.) Use a folded paper towel to apply a thin layer of soft butter to the pan. For decorative tube pans, a round pastry brush is a great tool for making sure that the butter gets into the crevices. If required, line the bottom of the pan with a round of parchment or wax paper cut to fit. As the parchment or wax paper is nonstick, there is no need to butter the round. Add about 2 tablespoons of all-purpose flour to the pan and tilt it to coat the inside of the pan with the flour. Turn the pan upside down and, over a garbage can or sink, tap out the excess flour. For fluted tube pans, see page 71 for a surefire way to prepare the pan and avoid sticking.

Be sure to sift the dry ingredients together. This easy step combines and aerates the ingredients so they are easier to mix into the batter (this is especially important with egg-based cakes, such as angel food or génoise). For the many recipes that use baking soda, which tends to clump, sifting pulverizes the leavening and distributes it well. For years, I thought it was sufficient merely to whisk the dry ingredients together, but I also had more than my share of cakes with little pellets of baking soda running through them. Sift the dry ingredients onto a large sheet of parchment or wax paper. When the time comes, use the parchment to lift the ingredients and pour them into the batter.

MIXING BUTTER CAKES

The procedure for mixing butter cakes hardly varies. The most important thing to remember is to beat plenty of air into the butter and sugar during the initial creaming. These bubbles are invisible, but they do an important job to keep the cake texture light.

Place the room-temperature butter in the bowl of a standing electric mixer fitted with the paddle blade. Beat at high speed until the butter is creamy and looks a shade paler, about 1 minute. At a steady pace (not too slowly), gradually beat in the sugar, about a tablespoon or so at a time, then continue beating until the butter and sugar are homogenous, very pale yellow, and light in texture (if not actually fluffy), about 3 minutes longer. Occasionally stop the mixer to scrape down the sides of the bowl with a rubber spatula. If you are using a hand mixer, allow about 4 minutes for the final stage of creaming the butter and sugar.

Now it's time to add the eggs. A familiar phrase in recipes occurs when adding the eggs to the batter: "one at a time, beating well after each addition." A cake batter is a carefully emulsified combination of disparate ingredients, and if one ingredient is added too quickly, the emulsion will break and the batter will look curdled. Even a single egg, which may not seem like such a large amount of liquid, can be enough to curdle a batter. Sometimes the curdling is corrected when the flour is added, but more often than not, it isn't and the result is tough cake. Adding room-temperature, beaten eggs to the batter is the best insurance against curdling. Beat the eggs together in a small bowl until well combined. With the mixer set on medium-high to high speed, add the beaten eggs slowly to the butter-and-sugar mixture, about a tablespoon at a time, and the emulsification will remain in check. (If the recipe calls for egg yolks only, they can be added without beating first.) Like the advice for sifting dry ingredients together, this little tip will immensely improve your cakes.

You are now ready to add the dry ingredients (the flour sifted with the leavening, salt, and possibly spices) to the mixture. The idea here is to add the dry and wet ingredients in stages so the batter stays emulsified. Add the dry ingredients in three additions, alternating with two additions of the liquids. The flour is always added first to strengthen the creamed butter and egg mixture. After each addition, beat until the batter looks smooth before adding the next portion. Occasionally stop the mixer to scrape down the sides of the bowl with a rubber or silicone spatula. (After the batter is smooth, some recipes call for folding in beaten egg whites to lighten the batter, which should be done by hand. In a separate bowl, using clean beaters, whip the whites until soft peaks form. Stir one-fourth of the whites into the batter to lighten it, then fold in the remaining whites.) At the end of mixing, fold in additional ingredients, such as nuts, dried fruit, or chocolate chips.

MIXING SPONGE CAKES

The crucial issue with sponge cakes is whipping the eggs to a foam that is stable enough to support the weight of the dry ingredients. If the eggs are underwhipped, the foam will not support the flour, and the cake will not rise. The usual description of this consistency is "light and fluffy," but "until it looks like old-fashioned aerosol shaving cream" is more accurate. The egg mixture will triple in volume and be very pale. When the beater is lifted an inch or so above the foam, the egg mixture should form a thick ribbon that falls back on itself and stays suspended on the surface of the foam for a few seconds before disappearing. This will take at least 3 minutes with a standing mixer, and about 5 minutes with a hand mixer.

For a génoise cake, the eggs and sugar are mixed together in a heatproof bowl and warmed over a saucepan of hot water before whipping. This extra step increases their elasticity and allows even more air bubbles to be beaten in. Be careful that the water does not touch the bottom of the bowl or the eggs could cook instead of warm. Again, allow plenty of time for the foam to reach the optimum consistency.

Once the egg foam is created, the dry ingredients are carefully sifted over the mixture and folded in. A large balloon whisk does this job well. You can also use a large rubber spatula, but the whisk's wires increase the flour's points of entry into the foam and combine the ingredients beautifully. Use a very light hand when folding, as the batter should remain as inflated as possible.

In génoise, melted butter is also added to the batter. The butter should be in a separate bowl and cooled until tepid. Transfer a large dollop of the batter to the butter, whisk them together until barely combined, then add this mixture to the batter and fold it in. If the butter were added by itself to the batter, it would sink to the bottom of the bowl and be difficult to fold in.

BAKING AND COOLING

Transfer the batter to the prepared pan(s) and spread it evenly with an offset spatula. To bake butter-based layers with the same height, use a kitchen scale to weigh equal amounts of the batter in each pan. (This assumes that the cake pans will be exactly the same model and weight, but that is usually the case.)

In most ovens, a single rack should be large enough to hold two cake pans. The pans should be spaced at least 2 inches apart and 2 inches from the sides of the oven. If your oven is small and the pans will be crowded, arrange a rack in the top third of the oven in addition to the center rack. Stagger the pans on the racks so they are not directly over each other. As heat rises, the cake on the top rack will bake more quickly than the center rack, so remove it as soon as it is done. Don't try to switch the positions of the cakes from top to bottom during baking, as the batter could deflate from the jostling.

Depending on the type of cake, there are different tests for doneness. First of all, even if you think your oven is accurate, check for doneness about 5 minutes before the estimated baking time has elapsed. Whether the cake is butter or sponge, the cake should be an appetizing golden brown. A properly baked butter cake will have shrunk slightly from the sides of the pan, and a wooden toothpick inserted in the center of the cake will come out clean. (For deep cakes baked in fluted pans, use a long bamboo skewer.) For a sponge cake, press the cake gently in the center—it should spring back.

Move butter cakes to wire cake racks and let cool in the pan for about 10 minutes. This allows the cake to set and cool slightly, but it still should be handled with care. Run a dull knife around the inside of the pan to loosen the cake from the pan. Place a rack over the pan, hold the two together, and invert. Remove the pan and carefully peel off the parchment or wax paper. Place a second rack over the cake and invert again so it is right side up. Let cool completely, at least 1 hour.

Sponge and génoise cakes are often cooled upside down, in the pans. Most pans have feet that lift the cake above the counter. Or balance the upside-down pan on three or four upturned coffee mugs of the same height. When the cake is cooled, run a metal icing spatula around the inside of the pan and the tube to loosen the cake. Remove the insert from the sides of the pan. Carefully pull the bottom of the cake away from the bottom of the insert (try not to use a knife to loosen it, as that would cut away the tasty exterior). Invert the loosened cake onto a serving platter, then remove the insert.

DECORATING CAKES

Butter cakes are baked in two separate layers that are sandwiched together with frosting or whipped cream. At least that is the approach that I have chosen for this book. Some bakers prefer to bake the batter in a single deep pan, and then cut the cake into layers. I have reserved that method for génoise. Some egg-rich cake recipes bake into layers with domed tops that need to be trimmed to make level layers, but none of the recipes in this book have that issue.

To cut a single cake into layers, determine the point where you want it split. Holding a serrated knife parallel to the work surface, make a shallow horizontal cut in the cake. Sawing with a gentle motion, and keeping the blade in the same position, turn the cake until it has made a complete rotation. Repeat turning and cutting the cake at the same incision, reaching deeper into the cake with the knife until you have cut completely through the cake. Slip a cardboard round under the cut layer and lift it off. You can apply this method to tall cakes, such as the chocolate génoise on page 119, to cut them into thirds.

Put a dab of the frosting in the center of a cardboard cake round. Place one cake layer, flat bottom side up, on the round. (Génoise cakes will need to be soaked with syrup before proceeding: Drizzle and brush about ½ cup of flavored syrup over the cake layer.) Scoop about ½ cup of the frosting onto the layer and spread evenly with a metal icing spatula.

Place the second layer, flat bottom side down, on the first layer. (Drizzle the génoise layer with the remaining syrup.) Place the cake on its cardboard round on the bottom of a wide, upturned bowl or coffee can so the cake can be turned as it is frosted. Spread a thin layer of the frosting, first over the top, then the sides, of the cake. Refrigerate until the frosting is set, about 10 minutes. This is called a "crumb coat," as it secures loose crumbs and readies the cake for a second layer of frosting. Now frost the cake with the remaining frosting, again starting with the top first and then the sides. There will be a ridge of frosting where the top meets the sides. To remove it, go around the perimeter of the cake with a series of short sweeping motions, smoothing the frosting from the edge toward the center.

To give your cake a finishing touch, a circle of piped frosting rosettes or swirls may be in order. Fit your pastry bag with a ½-inch diameter open star or French star pastry tip (such as Ateco #825 or #865). To fill the bag without an extra pair of hands, put the open bag into a tall drinking glass and fold the top of the bag over the sides of the glass like a cuff. Scoop the frosting into the bag, lift the bag out of the glass, and twist the end of the bag closed.

With one hand at the bottom of the bag, position the end of the tip about ½ inch above the surface of the cake. With the other hand, squeeze the frosting out of the bag. To make a simple six-pointed star shape, simply lift up the bag and stop applying pressure when the star is as big as you wish. (I estimate about 1 tablespoon of frosting per decoration to give you an idea of an appropriate size for most cakes.) For a swirl or rosette, move the pastry tip and bag in a tight circle as you pipe. If you wish, insert a final garnish, such as a chocolate-covered espresso bean or walnut half, into each piped decoration.

For cupcakes, the easiest method is to spread the top with a generous amount of frosting, using a small metal offset spatula. Or pipe large swirls of frosting on top of each cupcake for a look that would make your local bakery envious. Collect an arsenal of sprinkles, jimmies, and other miniature candies to add even more color, texture, and visual interest to your creations.

STORING AND SERVING

A cake dome will cover a layer cake and keep out air without marring the surface of the frosting. If you must use plastic wrap to cover the cake, insert a few wooden toothpicks in the top of the cake to keep the wrap from touching the frosting, then drape the wrap over the cake. Unfrosted cakes, such as coffee cakes, can simply be wrapped in plastic wrap.

Most cakes can be stored at room temperature for a day or two, keeping in mind that fresher is better. If you chose to refrigerate the cakes, keep in mind also that the butter in butter cakes will harden when chilled, so be sure to let them stand at room temperature for at least 2 hours before serving. Génoise and sponge cakes, which have relatively little butter in the batter, can be served chilled, but if you prefer soft frosting, remove them from the refrigerator for an hour or two before serving as well.

To slice frosted cakes, use a sharp, thin-bladed knife and a cake server to lift the slices. Spongy cakes, such as angel food, will slice more easily with a serrated knife. When storing sliced cake, press plastic wrap directly on its cut surfaces to prevent drying out.

COFFEE CAKES

By definition, a coffee cake seems destined to be served with coffee. Almost every coffee cake includes the familiar flavors of cinnamon, nuts, chocolate, and brown sugar, all of which are perfect partners for java. Coffee cakes are also fast and easy to make, encouraging impromptu invitations to friends and family to drop over for coffee and a slice of cake. Many a friendship has been created over a warm slice of homemade cake and a freshly brewed cup of coffee.

APPLE-CRANBERRY GINGER LOAF

Makes 8 servings

One bite of this applesauce cake brought me back to my childhood, when my grandmother would make such a treat for an afternoon coffee klatsch with her neighbors. In fact, it is based on a recipe from one of her recipe cards.

2 cups all-purpose flour, plus more for the pan

1 teaspoon baking soda

1 teaspoon ground cinnamon

½ teaspoon ground cloves

½ teaspoon salt

8 tablespoons (1 stick) unsalted butter, at room temperature, plus more for the pan

½ cup granulated sugar

½ cup packed light brown sugar

1 large egg, at room temperature

2 cups unsweetened applesauce

1 cup (4 ounces) coarsely chopped walnuts

1 cup dried cranberries or seedless raisins

⅓ cup finely chopped crystallized ginger

1. Position a rack in the center of the oven and preheat to 350°F. Lightly butter the inside of a 9 x 5-inch loaf pan. Line the bottom of the pan with wax paper and butter the paper. Dust the inside of the pan with flour and tap out the excess.

2. Sift the flour, baking soda, cinnamon, cloves, and salt together in a medium bowl . Beat the butter with an electric mixer set on high speed in a medium bowl until creamy, about 1 minute. Gradually beat in the sugars and continue beating, occasionally scraping down the sides of the bowl with a rubber spatula, until the mixture is light in color and texture, about 3 minutes. Beat in the egg. Reduce the mixer speed to low. In thirds, add the flour mixture, alternating with two equal additions of the applesauce, and mix until smooth, scraping down the sides of the bowl as needed. Stir in the walnuts, cranberries, and ginger. Pour into the pan and smooth the top.

3. Bake until a wooden toothpick inserted in the center of the cake comes out clean, 60 to 70 minutes. Let cool in the pan on a wire cake rack for 10 minutes. Run a knife around the inside of the pan to release the cake. Invert the cake onto the rack and remove the paper. Turn right side up and let cool completely. (The cake can be stored at room temperature, wrapped in aluminum foil, for up to 5 days.)

ALMOND BLUEBERRY BUCKLE

Makes 6 to 8 servings

Almond flour is the secret ingredient in this hard-to-surpass coffee cake, studded with juicy blueberries. It's just the thing to make for when company calls on a weekend morning. Almond flour has long been a secret ingredient of European pastry chefs, but it is now readily available at many American supermarkets and natural food stores. The reasonably priced Trader Joe's brand is made from unskinned almonds, and Bob's Red Mill brand is made from skinless nuts and is more expensive, but they are interchangeable in this recipe. (The almond flour with the skins may be too heavy for some batters.) Don't try to make your own almond flour in a food processor, as it will be too coarse.

1 cup all-purpose flour, plus more for the pan

¾ cup sugar

½ cup almond flour (also called almond meal)

2 teaspoons baking powder

½ teaspoon salt

½ cup whole milk

2 large eggs, at room temperature

4 tablespoons (½ stick) unsalted butter, well softened, plus more for the pan

½ teaspoon vanilla extract

¼ teaspoon almond extract

2 cups fresh or frozen blueberries

¼ cup sliced almonds

1. Position a rack in the center of the oven and preheat to 350°F. Lightly butter the inside of an 8-inch square metal baking pan. Dust the inside with flour and tap out the excess.

2. Whisk the flour, sugar, almond flour, baking powder, and salt together in a medium bowl. Add the milk, eggs, butter, vanilla, and almond extract. Using an electric mixer set on low speed, mix just until the ingredients are combined. Increase the mixer speed to high and beat, scraping the sides of the bowl often with a rubber spatula, for 2 minutes until the batter is smooth (use a timer). Stir in the blueberries. Spread the batter evenly in the pan. Sprinkle with the almonds.

3. Bake until a wooden toothpick inserted in the center of the cake comes out clean, 35 to 40 minutes. Transfer to a wire cake rack and let cool in the pan for at least 45 minutes. Serve warm or cool completely and serve at room temperature.

CINNAMON SWIRL COFFEE CAKE

Makes 10 to 12 servings

You can't have a collection of coffee cake recipes without including this iconic sour cream coffee cake. You know the one—cooked in a Bundt pan, with an interior swirl of nuts and cinnamon? Here's my version, which I have perfected over the years to have just the right balance of filling and batter, with a few other refinements.

Unflavored dried bread crumbs for the pan

2 cups all-purpose flour

½ teaspoon baking powder

½ teaspoon baking soda

½ teaspoon salt

1 cup (2 sticks) unsalted butter, at room temperature, plus more for the pan

1¾ cups granulated sugar

2 large eggs, beaten, at room temperature

1 teaspoon vanilla extract

1 cup full-fat sour cream, at room temperature

1 cup (4 ounces) chopped pecans or walnuts

2 tablespoons light brown sugar

2 teaspoons ground cinnamon

1. Position a rack in the center of the oven and preheat to 350°F. Lightly and evenly butter the inside of a 10-cup fluted tube pan, being sure to cover the crevices. Sprinkle in dried bread crumbs and tilt the pan to coat with the crumbs. Tap out the excess crumbs.

2. Sift the flour, baking powder, baking soda, and salt together in a medium bowl. Beat the butter in a large bowl with an electric mixer set at high speed until smooth, about 1 minute. Gradually beat in the granulated sugar, then continue beating, occasionally scraping down the sides of the bowl with a rubber spatula, until light in color and texture, about 3 minutes. Gradually beat in the eggs, then add the vanilla. In thirds, alternating with two equal additions of sour cream, add the flour, occasionally scraping down the sides of the bowl as needed, and beat until smooth.

3. Combine the pecans, brown sugar, and cinnamon together in a small bowl. Spread about one-third of the batter in the pan. Sprinkle in half of the pecan mixture, leaving a ½-inch border of batter around the outside edge of the pan. Spread with another third of the batter,

then sprinkle with the remaining pecan mixture. Top with the remaining batter and smooth the top.

4. Bake until a wooden skewer inserted in the center of the cake comes out clean, about 1 hour, 10 minutes. Let cool in the pan on a wire cake rack for 10 minutes. Invert onto the rack and remove the pan. Let cool for 30 minutes. Serve warm or cool completely and serve at room temperature.

A fluted cake irrevocably stuck in its pan is one of the worst things that can happen to a baker. There is a surefire solution to this problem: Do not coat the buttered pan with flour, but use dried bread crumbs instead. Whereas flour tends to soak into the batter, the crumbs act as a barrier.

Coat the interior of the pan with an even application of softened butter, being sure to get into the crevices of the design. A round-bristled pastry brush works best. Sprinkle in a few tablespoons of store-bought dried plain bread crumbs. Tilt the pan to completely coat the interior with the crumbs, then tap out the excess. Now pour in the batter. The baked cake will release with ease, showing off the pan's lovely pattern.

PEAR COFFEE CAKE
WITH STREUSEL CRUST

Makes 8 to 10 servings

My good friend and cookbook author Beth Hensperger and I often swap recipes in our e-mails to each other. Here's a coffee cake of the highest order from Beth, studded with big wedges of juicy pears. Don't expect a streusel topping—instead, the cinnamony crumble is pressed into the bottom of the pan to make a kind of crust. Beth advises firm-ripe pears for this cake, as soft ones will bake into mush.

Softened unsalted butter for the pan

2 cups all-purpose flour, plus more for the pan

2 cups packed light brown sugar

1 teaspoon ground cinnamon

1 teaspoon baking powder

½ teaspoon baking soda

½ teaspoon freshly ground nutmeg

½ teaspoon fine sea salt

8 tablespoons (1 stick) cold unsalted butter, cut into tablespoons

2 firm-ripe Bartlett or Bosc pears, each peeled, cored, and cut lengthwise into eighths

1 cup full-fat sour cream

1 large egg, at room temperature

1 teaspoon vanilla extract

1. Position a rack in the center of the oven and preheat to 350°F. Lightly butter and flour the inside of a 9-inch springform pan and tap out the excess flour.

2. Pulse the flour, brown sugar, cinnamon, baking powder, baking soda, nutmeg, and salt in a food processor fitted with the metal chopping blade to combine the ingredients. Add the butter and pulse about 20 times until the mixture forms fine crumbs. Do not process into large chunks.

3. Transfer 2½ cups of the crumb mixture to the pan and press it firmly and evenly into the bottom of the pan. Arrange the pear wedges side by side in a circle in the pan.

4. Whisk the sour cream, egg, and vanilla together in a small bowl. Add to the remaining crumb mixture in the food processor and process just until the batter is smooth; do not overmix. Spread evenly over the pears.

5. Bake until a wooden toothpick inserted in the center of the cake comes out clean and the cake is beginning to shrink from the sides of the pan, about 45 minutes. Transfer to a wire cake rack and let cool for 15 minutes. Run a knife around the inside of the pan, then remove the sides of the pan. Let cool until warm, about 1 hour. Serve warm or at room temperature.

PEACH KUCHEN

Makes 8 servings

When peaches are in season, you can't go wrong with this coffee cake, with slices of fruit peeking through the batter. It's a reliable recipe for just about any stone fruit, from cherries to nectarines (my grandmother used to make it with plums). This is another streusel-crowned cake, but you can replace that topping with a sprinkling of 1 tablespoon granulated sugar mixed with 1 teaspoon ground cinnamon.

KUCHEN

1⅓ cups all-purpose flour, plus more for the pan

1½ teaspoons baking powder

½ teaspoon salt

14 tablespoons (1¾ sticks) unsalted butter, at room temperature, plus more for the pan

1 cup granulated sugar

4 large eggs, beaten, at room temperature

1 teaspoon vanilla extract

3 ripe yellow or white peaches, peeled (see Note), pitted, and each cut into eighths

STREUSEL

½ cup all-purpose flour

¼ cup packed light brown sugar

½ teaspoon ground cinnamon

¼ teaspoon freshly grated nutmeg

4 tablespoons (½ stick) unsalted butter, at room temperature

1. Position a rack in the center of the oven and preheat to 350°F. Lightly butter the inside of an 11½ x 8-inch baking dish. Dust with flour and tap out the excess.

2. To make the kuchen, sift together the flour, baking powder, and salt in a medium bowl. Beat the butter in a medium bowl with an electric mixer on high speed until the butter is smooth, about 1 minute. Gradually beat in the sugar, then continue beating, occasionally scraping down

the sides of the bowl with a rubber spatula, until light and fluffy, about 3 minutes. Gradually beat in the eggs, then add the vanilla. Reduce the mixer speed to low. In thirds, add the flour mixture, mixing well after each addition and scraping down the sides of the bowl as needed. Spread the batter evenly in the pan. Arrange the peach slices in rows on top of the batter.

3. To make the streusel, combine the flour, brown sugar, cinnamon, and nutmeg together in a medium bowl. Add the butter and, using your fingers, rub the ingredients together until they form a soft dough. Crumble the dough in pea-size chunks evenly over the peaches.

4. Bake until a wooden toothpick inserted in the cake comes out clean, about 35 minutes. Let cool in the pan on a wire cake rack for 20 minutes. Cut into slices and serve warm, or let cool completely and serve at room temperature.

NOTE: To peel peaches, bring a medium saucepan of water to a boil over high heat. Add the peaches and heat just until the skins loosen, about 30 seconds. Drain and rinse the peaches under cold running water. Using a sharp knife, remove the skins.

CHOCOLATE CHIP CRUMB CAKE

Makes 8 servings

Any breakfast that includes chocolate improves vastly the prospects for the day ahead. This crumb cake, topped with a thick layer of cinnamon-accented crumble, isn't deeply chocolate, but it is studded with a good amount of chocolate chips. Use miniature chips, as large chips will sink in the batter.

CAKE

1½ cups all-purpose flour, plus more for the pan

2 teaspoons baking powder

⅛ teaspoon salt

½ cup whole milk

½ teaspoon vanilla extract

4 tablespoons (½ stick) unsalted butter, at room temperature, plus more for the pan

¾ cup granulated sugar

1 large egg, beaten, at room temperature

½ cup miniature chocolate chips

CRUMB TOPPING

2 cups all-purpose flour

12 tablespoons (1½ sticks) unsalted butter, at room temperature

½ cup packed light brown sugar

¼ cup granulated sugar

1 teaspoon ground cinnamon

1. Position a rack in the center of the oven and preheat to 350°F. Lightly butter and flour an 11½ x 8-inch baking dish and tap out the excess flour.

2. To make the cake, sift the flour, baking powder, and salt together in a medium bowl. Mix the milk and vanilla together in a glass measuring cup.

3. Beat the butter and sugar in a medium bowl with an electric mixer set at high speed until the mixture is light in color (it will look gritty, not fluffy), about 3 minutes. Beat in the egg. In

thirds, add the flour mixture, alternating with two equal additions of the milk mixture, beating after each addition and scraping the bowl as needed, until the batter is smooth. Stir in the chocolate chips. Scrape into the pan and smooth the top.

4. To make the crumb topping, combine the flour, butter, brown sugar, granulated sugar, and cinnamon in a medium bowl. Using your fingers, rub the ingredients together until they form a soft dough. Crumble the dough in pea-size chunks evenly over the batter.

5. Bake until the topping is firm and a toothpick inserted in the center of the cake comes out clean, about 40 minutes. Transfer to a wire cake rack and let cool. Cut and serve.

CUPCAKES FOR KIDS
OF ALL AGES

While cupcakes are sure to evoke memories of child-hood parties, these miniature cakes are no longer just for youngsters. Here's a tasty collection of cupcakes that features kid-friendly favorites, such as yellow cake with lots of buttercream icing, as well as the more sophisticated flavors of lemon and meringue.

BANANA-WALNUT CUPCAKES WITH CREAM CHEESE FROSTING

Makes 12 cupcakes

The old-fashioned flavor of banana cupcakes, especially when complemented by a big swirl of cream cheese frosting, is irresistible. While perfect as an afternoon snack, they also hit the mark when served for breakfast with your morning coffee. Be sure to use well-ripened, but not blackened, bananas. If the bananas sport lots of brown freckles, they are ripe enough.

BANANA-WALNUT CUPCAKES

1¼ cups all-purpose flour

1 teaspoon baking soda

½ teaspoon salt

8 tablespoons (1 stick) unsalted butter, at room temperature

1 cup granulated sugar

2 large eggs, beaten, at room temperature

3 well-ripened medium bananas, peeled and mashed (1 cup)

¾ cup finely chopped walnuts

CREAM CHEESE FROSTING

3 ounces cream cheese, at room temperature

2 tablespoons unsalted butter, at room temperature

1 teaspoon fresh lemon juice

¼ teaspoon vanilla extract

1¾ cups confectioners' sugar, sifted

1 or 2 teaspoons whole milk, if needed

Walnut halves for garnish

1. Position a rack in the center of the oven and preheat to 350°F. Line 12 cups in a muffin pan with paper cupcake liners.

2. To make the cupcakes, sift the flour, baking soda, and salt together in a medium bowl. Beat the butter in a large mixing bowl with an electric mixer set on high speed until the butter is

creamy, about 1 minute. Gradually beat in the sugar and beat until the mixture is light in color and texture, about 3 minutes. One at a time, beat in the eggs, scraping down the sides of the bowl. Beat in the mashed bananas. Reduce the mixer speed to low. In thirds, add the flour mixture, beating until the batter is smooth and scraping the bowl as needed. Fold in the nuts. Using an ice cream scoop with about ½ cup capacity, transfer the batter to the cups, filling each cup about three-fourths full.

3. Bake until a wooden toothpick inserted in the center of a cupcake comes out clean, about 25 minutes. Let cool in the pan on a wire cake rack for 10 minutes. Remove the cupcakes in their liners from the pan and let cool completely on the rack.

4. To make the frosting, beat the cream cheese and butter in a medium bowl with an electric mixer set on low speed until combined. Beat in the lemon juice and vanilla. Turn off the mixer and add half of the confectioners' sugar. Beat on low speed until smooth. Gradually beat in the remaining confectioners' sugar. Increase the speed to high and beat until the frosting is light and fluffy, about 1 minute longer. If the frosting is too thick, thin with a teaspoon or so of milk.

5. Transfer the frosting to a pastry bag fitted with a ½-inch open star tip, such as Ateco #825. Top each cupcake with a swirl of the frosting and a walnut half. (The cupcakes can be made 1 day ahead, stored under a cake cover at room temperature.)

BLACKOUT CUPCAKES

Makes 12 cupcakes

These cupcakes are triple-threat chocolate, with (chocolate) cake topped with (chocolate) icing, and encrusted with a coating of (chocolate) cake crumbs. Inspired by the blackout cakes popularized by Ebinger's, a long-closed and much-missed Brooklyn bakery, the exact recipe is the subject of much controversy among New York food lovers. My version has an ever-so-easy batter with a secret ingredient of its own, mayonnaise.

CHOCOLATE-MAYONNAISE CUPCAKES

2 cups all-purpose flour	1¼ cups sugar
⅓ cup plus 1 tablespoon natural cocoa powder	1 cup mayonnaise (not low fat)
2 teaspoons baking soda	1 cup strong brewed coffee, cooled
¼ teaspoon salt	1 teaspoon vanilla extract

CHOCOLATE GANACHE

1¼ cups heavy cream

10 ounces semisweet chocolate, finely chopped

1. Position a rack in the center of the oven and preheat to 350°F. Line 12 cups in a muffin pan with paper cupcake liners.

2. To make the cupcakes, sift the flour, cocoa, baking soda, and salt together into a large bowl. Add the sugar and whisk together. Whisk the mayonnaise, coffee, and vanilla in another large bowl until combined. Pour over the dry ingredients and whisk just until smooth. Using an ice cream scoop with about ½ cup capacity, transfer the batter to the cups, filling each cup about three-fourths full.

3. Bake until a wooden toothpick inserted in a cupcake comes out clean, 20 to 25 minutes. Let cool in the pan on a wire cake rack for 10 minutes. Remove the cupcakes in their liners from the pan and let cool completely on the rack.

4. Using a serrated knife, starting about ¼ inch below the top of each cupcake, trim off the domed tops. The idea here is simply to make a flat surface for the ganache topping—don't trim off too much cake or you'll have too many crumbs for the final garnish. Transfer the trimmings to a food processor and pulse to make coarse crumbs. Pour the crumbs into a bowl and set aside.

5. To make the ganache, heat the heavy cream in a saucepan over medium heat just until it comes to a simmer. Remove from the heat and add the chocolate. Let stand until the chocolate softens, about 3 minutes. Whisk until smooth.

6. Transfer the ganache to a medium bowl. Place the bowl in a larger bowl of ice water. Let stand, stirring and scraping the solidified portions of the ganache from the sides of the bowl, until the ganache is cool and about as thick as chocolate pudding, about 10 minutes. Remove the bowl from the ice and whisk just until the ganache forms soft peaks.

7. Transfer the ganache to a pastry bag fitted with a ½-inch plain pastry tip, such as Ateco #805. Pipe a mound of ganache on the top of each cupcake. Holding a cupcake over the bowl of crumbs, gently press the crumbs into the mound, covering it. (The cupcakes can be made 1 day ahead, covered and refrigerated. Remove from the refrigerator 1 hour before serving.) Serve at room temperature.

"BUTTERFLY" CUPCAKES

Whipped cream-and-preserves-filled cupcakes, decorated to look vaguely like butterflies, made an appearance at virtually every family party, and my cousins and I devoured them greedily every time. These sponge cupcakes were my favorite, but occasionally one of my aunties would use chocolate cupcakes (page 83), which are especially delicious with raspberry or strawberry preserves.

HOT MILK SPONGE CAKE

2 large eggs

1 cup cake flour (not self-rising)

1 teaspoon baking powder

¼ teaspoon salt

½ cup whole milk

2 tablespoons unsalted butter

1 cup granulated sugar

1 teaspoon vanilla extract

FILLING

¾ cup heavy cream

1 tablespoon confectioners' sugar

½ teaspoon vanilla extract

About ⅓ cup red currant, raspberry, or strawberry preserves

Confectioners' sugar for garnish

1. Position a rack in the center of the oven and preheat to 350°F. Line 12 cups in a muffin pan with paper cupcake liners.

2. To make the cupcakes, crack the eggs into a medium bowl. Place the bowl in a larger bowl of hot tap water. Let stand, stirring occasionally, until the eggs are warm to the touch, about 5 minutes.

3. Sift the flour, baking powder, and salt together in a medium bowl. Bring the milk and butter to a boil in a small saucepan over high heat. Reduce the heat to very low to keep the milk mixture hot.

4. Remove the bowl of eggs from the water. Add the sugar to the eggs and beat with an electric hand mixer set on high speed until the egg mixture is very light and pale yellow, 3 to 5 minutes. When the beaters are turned off and lifted an inch above the surface, the mixture should form a thick ribbon that falls back onto itself before dissolving. Sift the flour mixture over the beaten eggs and fold together with a wire whisk. Add the hot milk mixture and vanilla and whisk until the batter is smooth. Pour the batter (it will be thinner than most cake batters) into the cups, filling them almost, but not quite, full.

5. Bake until the cupcakes are golden brown and spring back when touched lightly on top, about 20 minutes. Let cool in the pan on a wire cake rack for 10 minutes. Remove the cupcakes in their liners from the pan and let cool completely on the rack.

6. To make the filling, whip the cream, confectioners' sugar, and vanilla in a bowl until stiff peaks form.

7. Using a small, sharp knife held at a diagonal, cut an inverted cone, with a base about 1½ inches wide, from the center of each cupcake. Keep track of which cone belongs to which cupcake. Cut each cone in half to make two wedge-shaped "butterfly wings."

8. Spoon an equal amount of whipped cream into the hole in each cupcake, then top with about 1 teaspoon of preserves. Perch the "wings" in the whipped cream. (The cupcakes can be made up to 8 hours ahead, covered loosely with plastic wrap and refrigerated.) Sift confectioners' sugar over the cupcakes and serve chilled.

LEMON MERINGUE CUPCAKES

Makes 12 cupcakes

If I was forced to choose my favorite pie (and please don't make me single out just one!), it might be lemon meringue. Inspired by a cake I saw at Tartine Bakery in San Francisco, and a batter from my friend Elinor Klivan's book *Cupcakes,* I have created a citrus cupcake with a tangy lemon filling and a swirl of tender meringue on top. Now I have a favorite cupcake to remind me of my beloved pie.

SOUR CREAM CUPCAKES

1¼ cups all-purpose flour

½ teaspoon baking powder

¼ teaspoon baking soda

¼ teaspoon salt

8 tablespoons (1 stick) unsalted butter,
at room temperature

1 cup sugar

Grated zest of 1 lemon

2 large eggs, beaten, at room temperature

½ cup sour cream, at room temperature

LEMON FILLING

⅓ cup plus 2 tablespoons sugar

2½ teaspoons cornstarch

½ cup fresh lemon juice

Pinch of fine sea salt

1 large egg plus 2 large egg yolks (save the
whites for the meringue)

2 tablespoons unsalted butter, thinly sliced

Grated zest of 1 lemon

MERINGUE

4 large egg whites, at room temperature   **½ cup sugar**

1. Position a rack in the center of the oven and preheat to 350°F. Line 12 cups in a muffin pan with paper cupcake liners.

2. To make the cupcakes, sift the flour, baking powder, baking soda, and salt together in a medium bowl. Beat the butter in another medium bowl with an electric mixer set on high speed until smooth, about 1 minute. Gradually beat in the sugar and then add the lemon zest. Beat until the mixture is light in color and texture, about 3 minutes. Gradually beat in the eggs. Reduce the speed to low. In halves, alternating with equal amounts of the sour cream, add the flour mixture, beating well after each addition and scraping down the sides of the bowl as needed. Using an ice cream scoop with about ½ cup capacity, transfer the batter to the cups, filling each cup about three-fourths full.

3. Bake until the cupcakes are golden brown and spring back when touched lightly on top, 20 to 25 minutes. Let cool in the pan on a wire cake rack for 10 minutes. Remove the cupcakes in their liners from the pan and let cool completely on the rack.

4. To make the filling, whisk the sugar and cornstarch together in a heavy-bottomed small saucepan. Whisk in the lemon juice and salt, then the egg and the egg yolks, and whisk well. Bring to a simmer over medium-low heat, whisking often. Reduce the heat to low and let bubble for 30 minutes. Strain through a medium-mesh sieve into a small bowl. Add the butter and lemon zest and stir until the butter melts. Press plastic wrap directly on the surface of the filling and pierce a few holes in the plastic. Let cool completely.

5. Using a small, sharp knife held at a diagonal, cut an inverted cone, with a base about 1½ inches wide, from the center of each cupcake. Discard the cones or reserve them as the baker's treat. Transfer the filling to a 1-quart plastic storage bag. Force the filling into one corner of the bag. Snip off the corner of the bag. Pipe an equal amount of the filling into the hole in each cupcake. Place the cupcakes on a baking sheet.

6. To make the meringue, preheat the oven to 375°F. Using clean beaters, beat the egg whites in a medium bowl with an electric mixer on high speed until soft peaks form. Gradually beat in the sugar and beat until the meringue forms stiff, shiny peaks. Transfer the meringue to a pastry bag fitted with a ½-inch French star tip, such as Ateco #865. (Any star tip will do, but a French tip gives the meringue an especially precise look.)

7. Pipe swirls of the meringue over the top of each cupcake, being sure that the filling is completely covered. Bake just until the meringue is tipped with brown, about 5 minutes. Let cool completely. The cupcakes are best served the day they are made.

PEANUT BUTTER CUPCAKES WITH MILK CHOCOLATE GANACHE

Makes 12 cupcakes

The combination of peanut butter and milk chocolate is sure to bring out the kid in everyone. To play up the whimsy, decorate the frosted tops with multicolored sprinkles, or maybe some chopped chocolate peanuts. A standard "old school" peanut butter works best in the batter—the all-natural ones make dense cupcakes.

PEANUT BUTTER CUPCAKES

2 cups all-purpose flour

2 teaspoons baking powder

¼ teaspoon baking soda

½ teaspoon salt

1 cup whole milk

½ teaspoon vanilla extract

½ cup chunky peanut butter

4 tablespoons (½ stick) unsalted butter, at room temperature

½ cup granulated sugar

¼ cup packed light brown sugar

2 large eggs, beaten

MILK CHOCOLATE GANACHE

¾ cup heavy cream

9 ounces milk chocolate, finely chopped

2 tablespoons unsalted butter, at room temperature

Multicolored sprinkles for garnish

1. Position a rack in the center of the oven and preheat to 350°F. Line 12 cups in a muffin pan with paper cupcake liners.

2. To make the cupcakes, sift the flour, baking powder, baking soda, and salt together in a medium bowl. Mix the milk and vanilla together in a glass measuring cup.

3. Beat the peanut butter and butter in a medium bowl with an electric mixer set at high speed until smooth, about 1 minute. Gradually beat in the sugars and beat until the mixture is light in color and texture, about 3 minutes. Gradually beat in the eggs. Reduce the mixer speed to low. In thirds, add the flour mixture, alternating with two equal additions of the milk mixture, beating until the batter is smooth and scraping the bowl as needed. Using an ice cream scoop with about ½ cup capacity, transfer the batter to the cups, filling each cup about three-fourths full.

4. Bake until a wooden toothpick inserted in the center of a cupcake comes out clean, about 25 minutes. Let the cupcakes cool in the pan on a wire cake rack for 10 minutes. Remove the cupcakes in their liners from the pan and let cool completely on the rack.

5. To make the ganache, bring the cream just to a simmer in a small saucepan over medium heat. Put the milk chocolate in a small heatproof bowl and pour the hot cream over the chocolate. Let stand until the chocolate softens, about 3 minutes, then whisk until smooth. Place the bowl in a larger bowl of ice water and let stand, stirring often with a rubber spatula, until cooled but not set, about 10 minutes. Remove the bowl from the water and add the butter to the ganache. Beat with an electric mixer on high speed until lightened in color and fluffy, about 1 minute.

6. Transfer the frosting to a pastry bag fitted with a ½-inch open star tip, such as Ateco #825. Top each cupcake with a swirl of the ganache and a scattering of sprinkles. (The cupcakes can be made 1 day ahead, stored under a cake cover at room temperature.)

RED VELVET CUPCAKES WITH FLUFFY FROSTING

Makes 20 cupcakes

With its meltingly tender crumb and shocking scarlet color, red velvet cake has lots of fans. There are a few caveats for the uninitiated. First, even though it contains cocoa, this is not a chocolate cake, and the cocoa is only in the batter to deepen the red color. Also, while many bakers (including this one) have used such ingredients as beets and raspberries to achieve the redness without resorting to food coloring, the visual results were lackluster: Food-coloring gel will give the deepest color. Add a crown of fluffy, marshmallowy frosting, and you'll be in cupcake heaven. This makes a lot of cupcakes, perfect for a party.

RED VELVET CUPCAKES

2½ cups all-purpose flour

2 tablespoons natural (not Dutch-processed) cocoa

1 teaspoon baking soda

½ teaspoon salt

1 cup buttermilk

1 tablespoon cider vinegar

1 teaspoon vanilla extract

1 cup (2 sticks) unsalted butter, at room temperature

1½ cups granulated sugar

2 large eggs, beaten, at room temperature

Red food-coloring gel or paste, as needed

Red decorating sugar for garnish

FLUFFY FROSTING

2 large egg whites, at room temperature

1½ cups superfine sugar

⅓ cup water

2 teaspoons corn syrup

¼ teaspoon cream of tartar

1 teaspoon vanilla extract

1. Position a rack in the center of the oven and preheat to 350°F. Line 20 muffin cups in 2 muffin pans with paper cupcake liners.

2. To make the cupcakes, sift the flour, cocoa, baking soda, and salt together in a medium bowl. Stir the buttermilk, vinegar, and vanilla together in a glass measuring cup.

3. Beat the butter in a large mixing bowl with an electric mixer on high speed until smooth, about 1 minute. Gradually beat in the sugar and beat until light in color and texture, about 3 minutes. Gradually beat in the beaten eggs, occasionally scraping down the sides of the bowl. Reduce the mixer speed to low. In thirds, add the flour mixture, alternating with two equal additions of the buttermilk mixture, beating well after each addition and scraping the bowl as needed. Beat in as much food coloring as needed to tint the batter vivid red. (The amount will vary with the type of coloring used—you may need only a few drops.) Using an ice cream scoop with about ½ cup capacity, transfer the batter to the cups, filling each cup about three-fourths full.

4. Bake until a wooden toothpick inserted in the center of a cupcake comes out clean, about 25 minutes. Let the cupcakes cool in the pans on wire cake racks for 10 minutes. Remove the cupcakes in their papers from the pans, and let cool completely on the racks.

5. To make the frosting, combine the egg whites, superfine sugar, water, corn syrup, and cream of tartar in a 2-quart double boiler insert or stainless steel bowl. Place the insert into a double boiler with briskly simmering water (the water should not touch the bottom of the insert) over medium heat. Using an electric mixer at high speed, beat until the frosting forms stiff, shiny peaks, about 6 minutes. Remove from the heat and beat in the vanilla. Use the frosting while it is still warm.

6. Using a metal icing spatula, top each cupcake with a billowing, generous dollop of the frosting. Sprinkle with the decorating sugar. (The cupcakes are best served on the day they are made.)

CLASSIC YELLOW CUPCAKES WITH BIG BUTTERCREAM FLOWERS

Makes 12 cupcakes

It seems that you can't walk into a New York City bakery these days without seeing a display of cupcakes decorated with a huge bouquet of colorful flowers made from buttercream frosting. They aren't hard to make at home. You will need a pastry bag and coupler fitted with a petal tip, such as Wilton #81. The buttercream is easy to make and work with, and is actually worth eating (something that cannot be said for the icing at most bakeries). You may have more buttercream than you need, but it allows for an extra helping of creativity.

YELLOW CAKE

1¼ cups cake flour (not self-rising)

1 teaspoon baking powder

⅛ teaspoon salt

3 tablespoons whole milk

½ teaspoon vanilla extract

10 tablespoons (1¼ sticks) unsalted butter, at room temperature

¾ cup sugar

3 large eggs, at room temperature, separated

BUTTERCREAM FROSTING

One 7½-ounce jar marshmallow creme

1½ cups (3 sticks) unsalted butter, at room temperature

1 teaspoon vanilla extract

Orange and yellow food-coloring paste

1. Position a rack in the center of the oven and preheat to 350°F. Line 12 cups in a muffin pan with paper cupcake liners.

2. To make the cake, sift the flour, baking powder, and salt together in a medium bowl. Mix the milk and vanilla together in a glass measuring cup. Beat the butter in a large bowl with an electric mixer set on high speed until the butter is smooth, about 1 minute. Gradually beat in

the sugar, then beat until the mixture is light in color and texture, about 3 minutes. One at a time, beat in the egg yolks. Reduce the mixer speed to low. In thirds, add the flour mixture, alternating with two equal additions of the milk mixture, beating well after each addition and scraping down the sides of the bowl as needed.

3. Using clean beaters, whip the egg whites in another large bowl with the mixer set on high speed until soft peaks form. Stir about one-fourth of the whites into the batter, then fold in the remaining whites. Using an ice cream scoop with about ½ cup capacity, transfer the batter to the cups, filling each cup about three-fourths full.

4. Bake until the cupcakes are golden brown and a wooden toothpick inserted in the center of a cupcake comes out clean, 20 to 25 minutes. Let the cupcakes cool in the pan on a wire cake rack for 10 minutes. Remove the cupcakes in their liners from the pan and let cool completely on the rack.

5. To make the buttercream frosting, place the marshmallow creme in a large mixing bowl. Beating with an electric mixer on medium speed, add the butter, 1 tablespoon at a time. Once all of the butter has been added, increase the speed to high and beat until the frosting is smooth and fluffy, about 1 minute. Beat in the vanilla.

6. Transfer about two-thirds of the frosting to a medium bowl. Using orange food-coloring paste, tint the frosting orange. Add a few drops of yellow food coloring and stir to create yellow streaks in the orange frosting. Transfer to a pastry bag fitted with a coupler and a small petal tip, such as Wilton #81.

7. Tint the remaining frosting yellow with the yellow food-coloring paste. Using a small metal icing spatula, spread a thin layer of yellow frosting on top of each cupcake. Transfer the remaining yellow frosting to a 1-quart plastic storage bag. Squeeze the frosting down to one corner of the bag. Snip off the corner of the bag.

8. For each cupcake, using the yellow frosting, pipe large dots of frosting in the center of the cupcake to cover an area about 1 inch in diameter. Starting at the perimeter of the dotted area and reaching the outer edge, use the orange frosting to pipe petals in a spoke pattern around the circumference of the cupcake. Finish with another layer of yellow dots in the center. (The cupcakes can be made up to 1 day ahead, stored under a cake cover.) Serve at room temperature.

ALL-AMERICAN
FAVORITES

These are the cakes that many of us grew up with: tender white cake, completely covered with fluffy icing and coconut shreds; deep, dark chocolate cake with intensely chocolate frosting; moist chiffon cake, tangy with citrus; light and tender angel food cake; aromatically spiced layer cake; and dense but creamy cheesecake. All of which, of course, would be delicious with coffee.

AMBROSIA COCONUT CAKE

Makes 8 servings

The salad known as ambrosia combines oranges, pineapple, coconut, and marshmallows. In my opinion, it makes a dubious salad, but these flavors work beautifully in a dessert. This cake features orange cake layers filled with pineapple, frosted with a fluffy frosting and coconut. It's just the kind of cake that you would expect to be served off a silver platter by a gracious Southern cook.

ORANGE CAKE

Softened unsalted butter and flour for the pans

2½ cups cake flour (not self-rising)

2½ teaspoons baking powder

¼ teaspoon baking soda

¼ teaspoon salt

½ cup whole milk

½ cup fresh orange juice

8 tablespoons (1 stick) unsalted butter, at room temperature

Grated zest of 1 orange

1¼ cups granulated sugar

2 large eggs, beaten, at room temperature

PINEAPPLE FILLING

One 8-ounce can crushed pineapple in pineapple juice

½ cup canned pineapple juice (in addition to the juice drained from the crushed pineapple), as needed

4 teaspoons cornstarch

1 tablespoon granulated sugar

FLUFFY FROSTING

1 cup superfine sugar

3 tablespoons water

1 large egg white

1 tablespoon light corn syrup

Pinch of salt

⅛ teaspoon cream of tartar

½ teaspoon vanilla extract

1½ cups sweetened flaked coconut

1. Position a rack in the center of the oven and preheat to 350°F. Lightly butter two 8 x 1½-inch round cake pans and line the bottoms with wax or parchment paper. Dust with flour and tap out the excess.

2. To make the cake, sift the flour, baking powder, baking soda, and salt together in a medium bowl. Mix the milk and orange juice together. Beat the butter and orange zest together in a large bowl with an electric mixer on high speed until smooth. Gradually beat in the sugar, then continue beating until the mixture is light in color and texture, about 3 minutes. Gradually beat in the beaten eggs. Reduce the mixer speed to low. In thirds, add the flour mixture, alternating with two equal additions of the milk mixture, scraping down the sides of the bowl as needed, and beat until smooth. Divide equally between the cake pans and spread evenly.

3. Bake until a wooden toothpick inserted in the center of the cakes comes out clean, 20 to 25 minutes. Transfer the pans to wire cake racks and let cool for 10 minutes. Invert the cakes onto the racks, remove the pans and paper, turn right sides up, and cool completely.

4. To make the filling, drain the pineapple in a wire sieve set over a glass measuring cup; press gently to extract the excess juice. You should have about ⅓ cup. Add additional pineapple juice to make ¾ cup. Sprinkle the cornstarch over the juice and whisk to dissolve. Transfer to a small saucepan. Add the drained pineapple and sugar; stir well. Continue stirring over medium-low heat until the mixture comes to a full boil, about 3 minutes. Transfer to a bowl and let cool completely.

5. To make the frosting, whisk the superfine sugar, water, egg white, corn syrup, salt, and cream of tartar together in the top part of a double boiler. Place over a saucepan of briskly simmering water. Beat with an electric mixer on high speed until the frosting forms stiff, shiny peaks, 5 to 7 minutes. Remove from the heat and beat in the vanilla.

6. Place a dab of frosting in the center of a 7-inch cardboard cake round. Place one cake layer, flat side up, on the round. Spread with the cooled pineapple filling. Place the other cake layer, flat side down, on the filling. Spread with the frosting, first the top and then the sides. Gently press handfuls of the coconut all over the cake. Slice and serve.

NOTE: If you don't have superfine sugar, grind 1 cup granulated sugar in a food processor or blender until it is very fine, about 2 minutes.

ANGEL FOOD CAKE
WITH COFFEE CREAM

Makes 10 servings

Angel food cake is known for its ethereal texture and delicate flavor. I have memories of it from my childhood, when it was served at parties with generous dollops of whipped cream. In addition to moistening the cake, the cream was also scooped into the accompanying cups of coffee to act as a Viennese-style coffee lightener. As a nod to these reminiscences, coffee flavors the whipped cream in this recipe.

ANGEL FOOD CAKE

1 cup cake flour (not self-rising)

1¼ cups superfine sugar, divided

¼ teaspoon salt

12 large egg whites, at room temperature

1 teaspoon cream of tartar

1 teaspoon vanilla extract

COFFEE CREAM

1½ cups heavy cream

2½ teaspoons instant espresso powder

3 tablespoons confectioners' sugar

1. To make the cake, position a rack in the center of the oven and preheat to 350°F.

2. Sift the flour, ¾ cup of the superfine sugar, and the salt together in a medium bowl. Beat the egg whites in a large bowl with an electric mixer set on low speed until foamy. Add the cream of tartar and increase the speed to high. Beat until the whites form soft peaks. A tablespoon at a time, add in the remaining ½ cup superfine sugar and beat until the whites form stiff, shiny peaks. Add the vanilla.

3. In thirds, sift the flour mixture over the whites and fold together, using a large balloon whisk or rubber spatula. Transfer the batter to an ungreased 10-inch round tube pan (not nonstick) with a removable bottom and smooth the top.

4. Bake until the cake is golden brown and it springs back when pressed, about 1 hour. Set the cake in its pan upside down on a work surface. The cake must clear the counter—balance the edges of the pan on three equally spaced coffee mugs if necessary. Cool completely.

5. To make the coffee cream, pour the cream into a medium bowl and sprinkle in the espresso powder. Refrigerate until the espresso powder softens, about 15 minutes. Add the confectioners' sugar. Whip with an electric mixer set on high speed until soft peaks form. Cover and refrigerate until serving.

6. Run a long, thin knife around the inside edge and tube of the pan. Invert the pan and remove the sides. Carefully pull the cake from the bottom of the tube insert and remove the cake.

7. Place the cake on a serving platter. Using a serrated knife, cut into slices and serve, adding a generous dollop of the coffee cream to each serving.

DAIQUIRI CHIFFON CAKE

Savvy bakers make chiffon cakes an important part of their repertoire. Not only are these cakes utterly delicious and versatile (see the limoncello variation), they are good keepers and stay moist and tender for longer than many other cakes. Here is one of my favorites, fragrant with lime and rum. Golden rum works best for baking, as clear (known as light or silver) rums are too delicately flavored, and dark rums often have an undesirable caramel overtone.

CAKE

3 limes

¼ cup golden rum

2¼ cups cake flour (not self-rising)

1½ cups granulated sugar

1 tablespoon baking powder

1 teaspoon salt

½ cup canola or vegetable oil

5 large eggs, separated, plus 3 large egg whites, at room temperature

1 teaspoon vanilla extract

½ teaspoon cream of tartar

ICING

2 cups confectioners' sugar

2 tablespoons golden rum

1 tablespoon fresh lime juice

1. Position a rack in the center of the oven and preheat to 350°F.

2. To make the cake, grate the zest from 2 limes and set aside. Juice the limes; you should have at least ⅓ cup. Combine ¼ cup of the lime juice with ¼ cup water and the rum. Set the lime mixture and remaining lime juice aside.

3. Sift the flour, sugar, baking powder, and salt together in a large bowl. Make a well in the center of the dry ingredients and add, in this order, the oil, 5 egg yolks, lime-rum mixture, lime zest, and vanilla. Mix with an electric mixer on low speed just until the batter is smooth, scraping down the sides of the bowl often.

4. Combine the 8 egg whites and cream of tartar in another large bowl. Using clean beaters, whip with the mixer set on high speed just until stiff peaks form. Stir about one-fourth of the whites into the batter to lighten it, then fold in the remaining whites with a rubber spatula. Pour into an *ungreased* 10-inch diameter tube pan with a removable bottom. Smooth the top of the batter.

5. Bake until the cake springs back when pressed on top with a finger, about 50 minutes. Invert the cake pan onto a work surface and let the cake cool completely. (If the upside-down pan does not balance on its own, set the edges of the pan on upturned ramekins.)

6. Run a long metal spatula or thin knife around the inside of the pan and tube to loosen the cake. Remove the cake from the pan, then carefully pull the bottom of the cake away from the insert. Place the cake, smooth side up, on a wire cake rack set over a rimmed baking sheet.

7. To make the icing, sift the confectioners' sugar into a medium bowl. Add the rum and 1 table-spoon of the reserved lime juice and stir until smooth. Add enough water to make a thick icing with the consistency of heavy cream, about 2 teaspoons. Drizzle the icing over the cake, letting the excess run down the sides. Let stand until the icing sets, about 1 hour. (The cake can be made up to 3 days ahead, wrapped in plastic wrap and stored at room temperature.) Slice and serve.

LIMONCELLO CAKE In the cake, substitute lemons for the limes and limoncello liqueur for the rum, and lemon juice for the lime juice in the icing.

CHOCOLATE CAKE WITH CHOCOLATE MALT FROSTING

Makes 10 servings

For just about any occasion that calls for cake, you simply cannot go wrong with chocolate, particularly this rich and satisfying layer cake put together with a malted milk frosting. One of the secrets to a top-notch chocolate cake is to use cocoa, not chocolate, and to combine the powder with boiling water to turn it into a puddinglike paste that permeates the dark batter. Be sure to use natural, not Dutch-processed, cocoa for this recipe, so it can react with the baking soda to help the cake rise. (Dutch-processed cocoa has been alkalized to reduce the acidity of the cocoa, and won't create the necessary chemical reaction.) For a decorating variation, skip piping frosting rosettes on the cake and arrange extra malted milk balls around its perimeter.

CHOCOLATE CAKE

1 cup boiling water

¾ cup natural (not Dutch-processed) cocoa powder

1¾ cups all-purpose flour

1½ teaspoons baking soda

¼ teaspoon salt

1½ cups buttermilk, at room temperature

1 teaspoon vanilla extract

10 tablespoons (1¼ sticks) unsalted butter, at room temperature

2 cups granulated sugar

3 large eggs, beaten

CHOCOLATE MALT FROSTING

4 ounces unsweetened chocolate, chopped

⅓ cup whole milk, plus more as needed

¼ cup unflavored or chocolate malted milk powder

8 tablespoons (1 stick) unsalted butter, at room temperature

1 teaspoon vanilla extract

3¾ cups (1 pound) confectioners' sugar, sifted, plus more as needed

1 cup malted milk balls

1. Position a rack in the center of the oven and preheat to 350°F. Lightly butter two 9 x 1½-inch round cake pans and line the bottoms with wax or parchment paper. Dust with flour and tap out the excess.

2. To make the cake, whisk the boiling water and cocoa together in a medium bowl until smooth. Let cool completely.

3. Sift the flour, baking soda, and salt together in a medium bowl. Mix the buttermilk and vanilla together. Beat the butter in a medium bowl with an electric mixer set on high speed until smooth. Gradually beat in the sugar. Beat until the mixture is light in color and texture, about 3 minutes. Gradually beat in the beaten eggs. Beat in the cooled cocoa mixture. Reduce the mixer speed to low. In thirds, add the flour mixture, alternating with two equal additions of the buttermilk, scraping down the sides of the bowl as needed, and beat until smooth. Divide equally between the cake pans and spread evenly.

4. Bake until a wooden toothpick inserted in the center of the cakes comes out clean, 30 to 35 minutes. Transfer the pans to wire cake racks and let cool for 10 minutes. Invert the cakes onto the racks, remove the pans and paper, turn right sides up, and cool completely.

5. To make the frosting, melt the chocolate in the top part of a double boiler set over hot, not simmering, water. Remove from the heat and let cool until tepid.

6. Whisk the milk and malted milk powder together to dissolve the powder. Combine the butter, cooled chocolate, and vanilla in a large bowl. Add half of the confectioners' sugar. Mix with an electric mixer on low speed, gradually adding the remaining confectioners' sugar, alternating with the milk mixture, until the frosting is smooth. If the frosting is too thick, thin with additional milk. If the frosting is too thin, add more confectioners' sugar. Beat on high speed until light and fluffy, about 1 minute.

7. Reserve 10 of the malted milk balls to garnish. Coarsely chop the remaining balls in a food processor fitted with the metal blade.

8. Place a dab of frosting in the center of a 7-inch cardboard cake round. Transfer about ½ cup of the frosting to a pastry bag fitted with a ½-inch star tip, such as Ateco #825. Place one

cake layer, flat side up, on the round. Spread with ½ cup of the frosting, then sprinkle with the chopped malted milk balls. Place the other cake layer, flat side down, on the filling. Spread with the frosting, first the top, and then the sides. Using the frosting in the pastry bag, pipe 10 rosettes around the top edge of the cake, and place a malted milk ball in each rosette. Slice and serve.

SPICE LAYER CAKE WITH PRALINE FROSTING

Makes 8 to 10 servings

My Southern friends tout caramel cake, a popular yellow cake with boiled sugar frosting that is often served at family events, such as christenings and funerals, as one of their favorites. Here is my take, with spice cake layers and a simplified icing, and the additional fillip of chopped pecans. The frosting is as rich as they come, so I find that a thin layer is sufficient, but you can increase the ingredients by half if you prefer a thick coating.

SPICE CAKE

Softened unsalted butter and flour for the pans

2½ cups all-purpose flour

1 teaspoon baking powder

1 teaspoon baking soda

1 teaspoon ground cinnamon

½ teaspoon ground ginger

½ teaspoon ground cloves

½ teaspoon salt

¼ teaspoon freshly ground black pepper

8 tablespoons (1 stick) unsalted butter, at room temperature

1 cup granulated sugar

¾ cup packed light brown sugar, rubbed through a sieve to remove lumps

3 large eggs, beaten, at room temperature

1 teaspoon vanilla extract

1⅓ cups buttermilk, at room temperature

PRALINE FROSTING

8 tablespoons (1 stick) unsalted butter

1 cup packed light brown sugar

¼ cup plus 2 tablespoons buttermilk, as needed

2 cups confectioners' sugar, sifted

1 teaspoon vanilla extract

1 cup (4 ounces) finely chopped pecans for garnish

1. Position a rack in the center of the oven and preheat to 350°F. Lightly butter two 9 x 1½-inch round cake pans and line the bottoms with wax or parchment paper. Dust with flour and tap out the excess.

2. To make the cake, sift the flour, baking powder, baking soda, cinnamon, ginger, cloves, salt, and pepper together in a medium bowl. Beat the butter in a large bowl with an electric mixer on high speed until smooth, about 1 minute. Gradually beat in the granulated sugar and brown sugar, then continue beating until the mixture is light in color and texture, about 3 minutes. Gradually beat in the beaten eggs, occasionally scraping down the sides of the bowl, then the vanilla. Reduce the mixer speed to low. In thirds, add the flour mixture, alternating with two equal additions of the buttermilk, occasionally scraping down the sides of the bowl, and beat until smooth. Divide equally between the cake pans and spread evenly.

3. Bake until a wooden toothpick inserted in the center of the cakes comes out clean, about 30 minutes. Transfer the pans to wire cake racks and let cool for 10 minutes. Invert the cakes onto the racks, remove the pans and paper, turn right sides up, and cool completely.

4. To make the frosting, melt the butter in a heavy-bottomed medium saucepan over medium heat. Whisk in the brown sugar and whisk until melted. Reduce the heat to medium-low and let bubble, whisking constantly, for 2 minutes. Whisk in ¼ cup of the buttermilk and boil for 15 seconds. Remove from the heat and let stand until tepid, about 30 minutes.

5. Using an electric mixer set on low speed, gradually beat in the confectioners' sugar, using a rubber spatula to scrape up and incorporate the brown sugar mixture in the corners of the saucepan. Beat in the vanilla. Gradually beat in enough of the remaining buttermilk to bring the frosting to a spreadable consistency, about 2 tablespoons. Increase the speed to high and beat until the frosting is light and fluffy, about 1 minute.

6. Place a dab of frosting in the center of an 8-inch cardboard cake round. Place one cake layer, flat side up, on the round. Spread with ½ cup of the frosting. Place the other cake layer, flat side down, on the filling. Spread the cake, first the top, then the sides, with the remaining frosting. Press the pecans onto the sides of the cake. (The cake can be made up to 1 day ahead, stored at room temperature and covered with a cake cover.) Slice and serve.

S'MORES CHEESECAKE

Makes 12 servings

Indulge in this very grown-up version of the childhood favorite. It is also quite sweet, so a bracing cup of coffee will be welcome to help balance the sweetness. I like to serve it at the end of a summer barbecue with tall glasses of iced coffee. A kitchen torch comes in handy to give the marshmallow topping an even color, but the toasting can be done in a broiler as well.

CRUST

Softened unsalted butter for the pan

1½ cups graham cracker crumbs

3 tablespoons sugar

6 tablespoons (¾ stick) unsalted butter, melted

FILLING

9 ounces milk chocolate, coarsely chopped

1 pound cream cheese, softened

¾ cup sugar

⅛ teaspoon salt

¾ cup heavy cream, at room temperature

3 large eggs, at room temperature

TOPPING

1 cup sugar

2 large egg whites

1 teaspoon cream of tartar

⅛ teaspoon salt

12 large marshmallows, snipped into quarters with wet scissors

½ teaspoon vanilla extract

1. Position a rack in the center of the oven and preheat to 350°F. Lightly butter the inside of a 9-inch springform pan.

2. To make the crust, stir together the cracker crumbs, sugar, and melted butter to moisten in a medium bowl. Press firmly and evenly into the bottom and ¼ inch up the sides of the pan.

Bake until lightly toasted and fragrant, 12 to 15 minutes. Remove from the oven. Reduce the oven temperature to 325°F.

3. To make the filling, melt the chocolate in the top part of a double boiler over very hot, not simmering, water, stirring occasionally, until smooth. Remove from the heat and cool until tepid.

4. In a food processor, process the cream cheese, sugar, and salt together until smooth, stopping to scrape down the sides of the work bowl with a rubber spatula. With the machine running, add the cream and then stop it to scrape down the bowl. With the machine running again, add the chocolate, then the eggs, one at a time, processing and scraping until the mixture is smooth. Pour into the crust.

5. Bake until the sides of the cheesecake are slightly risen and the cheesecake looks set (the very center of the filling will look shiny and unset), about 1 hour. Transfer to a wire cake rack. Run a wet, sharp knife around the inside of the pan to loosen the cheesecake from the sides. Let cool completely.

6. Cover the cheesecake with plastic wrap and refrigerate until chilled, at least 4 hours. (The cheesecake can be refrigerated for up to 1 day.)

7. To make the topping, combine the sugar, egg whites, 3 tablespoons water, the cream of tartar, and salt in the top part of a double boiler or a heatproof bowl. Place over a saucepan of simmering water and whisk until the sugar dissolves and the mixture is hot and opaque, about 2 minutes. Remove from the heat and add the marshmallows to the sugar mixture. Let stand to soften the marshmallows, about 3 minutes. Return to the simmering water and beat with an electric hand mixer set on high speed until the topping stands in stiff, shiny peaks, about 5 minutes. Beat in the vanilla.

8. Unwrap the cheesecake and remove the sides of the pan. Using a metal icing spatula, spread the topping over the cheesecake, swirling it in peaks. Let stand until cooled and set, about 15 minutes.

9. Using a kitchen torch, wave the flame over the cheesecake until lightly browned. Or broil the cheesecake in a preheated broiler about 4 inches from the source of heat until lightly browned, about 1 minute. (The marshmallow-topped cheesecake can be refrigerated for up to 1 day.) Using a sharp, thin knife rinsed under hot water, cut into slices and serve.

Tips on Cheesecakes

Cheesecakes are blatantly indulgent and sinful—there have been times when I put one on the table and my guests have actually cheered! When I have a large group to serve, a cheesecake is often my first choice, because I get a lot of servings with a minimum of effort. As easy as cheesecakes are to make, here are a few tips to ensure that yours will be creamy smooth and without any surface cracks.

• To avoid lumps in the batter, be sure the cream cheese is well softened before mixing. Remove the cheese from its wrapper and cut into chunks. Place in the mixing bowl, loosely cover with plastic wrap, and let stand for at least 2 hours at room temperature.

• Overbeating is a common problem with cheesecakes. If too much air is beaten into the batter, it will "soufflé" (puff up and fall) in the oven, leading to cracks and a spongy texture. A food processor will not incorporate as much air as an electric mixer, so the processor has become my mixing tool of choice for cheesecakes. Just stop the machine occasionally to scrape down the sides and fully incorporate the cream cheese.

• Cheesecake filling is very closely related to custard—eggs mixed with dairy products and baked. Overbaked custard will separate and be watery, and the same fate can await an overbaked cheesecake. An oven temperature over 325°F encourages curdling. I preheat the oven to 350°F for an initial burst of heat, but then I reduce the temperature to 325°F as soon as the cheesecake goes into the oven.

• Cracks are the bane of the cheesecake baker's existence. If the filling is stuck to the sides of the pan, the cake will pull apart and crack while it cools and contracts. To fix this problem, as soon as the cheesecake comes out of the oven, run a wet, sharp knife around the inside of the pan to loosen the cake from the sides. Cool the cake on a rack in a draft-free place. Some bakers find the oven itself (with the door held ajar with a wooden spoon to release heat) to be the ideal cooling place, but my oven is usually in use, so I just cool the cheesecake on a cake rack on the kitchen counter. Don't rush cooling by putting the hot cake in a cold place (such as the freezer, refrigerator, or even a cold porch in the winter), as the shock in temperature differences can also cause cracking. S'mores Cheesecake has a topping, so cracks aren't an issue, but cracking is the sign of a poorly made cheesecake, so get into the habit of using these tips and you'll never have that onus.

EUROPEAN CAFÉ TREATS

I know I'm not the only one who plans his travel itinerary according to the location of the best bakeries, coffeehouses, and cafés. These desserts represent some of my favorites from trips over the years. A bite of any one of them will instantly transport me back to Europe, sitting at a café with a cup of coffee by my side.

BLACK FOREST CAKE

Makes 8 servings

There used to be countless German cafés and bakeries in New York City's Yorkville district of the Upper East Side. Black Forest cake, a rococo chocolate and whipped cream extravaganza featuring cherries and a heady dose of kirsch, was proudly served at every one of these places. As the European immigrant population has dwindled, so has the frequency of Black Forest cake sightings. Here it is, restored to glory. It is a long recipe, not particularly difficult, and worth every bit of effort. If you can find them, use sour cherries instead of sweet for the true European flavor. I recommend canned cherries here, as I have never had a Black Forest cake made with fresh cherries, and fresh sour cherries have a limited availability during their short season.

CHOCOLATE GÉNOISE

Softened unsalted butter
for the pan

¾ cup granulated sugar

4 large eggs

⅔ cup cake flour (not self-rising),
plus more for the pan

¼ cup Dutch-processed or
natural cocoa powder

⅛ teaspoon fine sea salt

3 tablespoons whole milk

3 tablespoons vegetable oil

½ teaspoon vanilla extract

CHERRY FILLING

One 14.5-ounce can tart, sour, or sweet
cherries in juice, well drained, juices reserved

2½ teaspoons cornstarch

3 tablespoons granulated sugar

KIRSCH SYRUP

½ cup granulated sugar

⅓ cup kirsch (see Note)

WHIPPED CREAM

2 teaspoons unflavored powdered gelatin

2½ cups heavy cream

3 tablespoons confectioners' sugar

1 teaspoon vanilla extract

One 4- to 5-ounce chunk of semisweet or bittersweet chocolate

1. Position a rack in the center of the oven and preheat to 350°F. Lightly butter the inside of an 8 x 3-inch springform pan. Line the bottom with a round of wax paper. Dust the inside of the pan with flour and tap out the excess.

2. To make the génoise, bring a medium saucepan with 1 inch of water to a brisk simmer over high heat. Reduce the heat to medium-low to maintain the simmer. Whisk the sugar and eggs together in the bowl of a heavy-duty standing mixer. Place over the simmering water (the bowl should not touch the water) and whisk constantly until the sugar is dissolved and the egg mixture is hot (dip in your finger), about 2 minutes. Attach the bowl to the mixer and fit with the whisk attachment. Beat on high speed until the mixture has tripled in volume and is very pale and fluffy, about 4 minutes. (You can use a large heatproof bowl and a hand mixer to prepare the egg mixture, but allow at least 5 minutes of beating.)

3. Meanwhile, sift the flour, cocoa, and salt together and set aside. Heat the milk and oil together in a small saucepan or in a microwave oven until steaming. Transfer to a medium bowl, add the vanilla, and set aside.

4. Remove the bowl from the mixer. In thirds, sift the flour mixture over the egg mixture and fold it in with a large balloon whisk or a rubber spatula. Transfer about one-fourth of the batter to the milk mixture in the bowl and whisk together to combine. Return this mixture to the batter and fold it in. Pour into the pan and smooth the top.

5. Bake until the top of the cake springs back when lightly pressed in the center with your fingers, 30 to 35 minutes. Let cool in the pan on a wire cake rack for 10 minutes. Run a sharp knife around the inside of the pan to release the cake. Invert the cake onto the rack and remove the pan bottom and wax paper. Turn right side up and let cool completely.

6. To make the filling, set aside 8 of the drained cherries for garnish. You should have about 1⅓ cups cherries. Measure the juice; you should have ⅔ cup; add water if needed. Pour the juice into a small saucepan. Add the cornstarch and stir to dissolve. Stir in the sugar. Bring to a boil over medium heat, stirring constantly. Remove from the heat and stir in the cherries. Transfer to a bowl and let cool completely.

7. To make the kirsch syrup, combine the sugar and ½ cup water in a small saucepan. Bring to a boil over high heat, stirring constantly to dissolve the sugar. Reduce the heat to low and simmer for 30 seconds. Remove from the heat and let cool completely. Stir in the kirsch.

8. To make the whipped cream, sprinkle the gelatin over 3 tablespoons cold water in a ramekin or custard cup. Let stand until the gelatin soaks up the water, about 5 minutes. Bring about ¼ inch of water to a simmer in a skillet over medium heat. Place the ramekin in the skillet and turn off the heat. Stir until the gelatin is completely dissolved, about 1 minute. Remove the ramekin from the water. Add 2 tablespoons of the heavy cream to the dissolved gelatin and stir. (The gelatin will stabilize the whipped cream and keep it from weeping before serving.)

9. Combine the remaining cream, the cream-gelatin mixture, confectioners' sugar, and vanilla in a chilled medium bowl. Whip the cream with an electric mixer on high speed until stiff.

10. Using a long serrated knife, cut the cake horizontally into three equal layers. Place the top layer (with the "skin"), cut side up, on an 8-inch cardboard cake round. Brush about ⅓ cup of the kirsch syrup over the cake layer. Spread with about ¾ cup of the whipped cream, making a 1-inch-wide border around the perimeter of the layer that is slightly higher than the cream in the center. Spread half of the cherry filling in the center of the cream layer, letting the cream border contain the filling. Repeat with another cake layer, syrup, cream, and the remaining filling. Top with the final cake layer and brush with the remaining syrup.

11. Spread the top and sides of the cake with a thin layer of the whipped cream, just enough to mask the cake and its crumbs. Refrigerate the cake (but not the bowl of cream) until the cream is set, about 10 minutes.

12. Transfer 1 cup of the whipped cream to a pastry bag fitted with a ½-inch star tip, such as Ateco #825, and set aside. Spread the top and then the sides of the cake with the remaining

cream. Pipe 8 equally spaced rosettes around the top perimeter of the cake and insert one of the reserved cherries in each rosette.

13. Heat the chocolate in a microwave oven on medium power for 20 seconds. The exterior of the chocolate should be very slightly softened—it will be hardly perceivable. Working over a piece of wax or parchment paper, using a vegetable peeler and firm pressure, shave chocolate curls from the flat side of the chocolate chunk. You will only need about half of the chocolate. Scatter the chocolate curls from the wax paper over the top of the cake. (Do not touch the curls with your fingers or the curls will melt.)

14. Refrigerate the remaining chocolate to firm it, about 15 minutes. Grate the chocolate on the large holes of a box grater into a small bowl. With one hand, hold the cake over a baking sheet, tilting the cake slightly. With a large metal spoon in your other hand, scoop up the grated chocolate and scatter it over the sides of the cake. (Do not touch the chocolate with your fingers or it will melt.) Save any grated chocolate that doesn't adhere for another use.

15. Refrigerate until the cream is set, at least 1 hour or overnight. Slice with a sharp, thin-bladed knife and serve chilled.

NOTE: Kirsch (also called kirschwasser) is a clear cherry eau-de-vie with a bracing, if not very cherrylike, flavor. It was originally made from morello cherries, a type of sour cherry grown in the Black Forest region of Germany, but now other varieties are also used. (And now you know how Black Forest cake got its name!) Top-notch kirsch is always expensive because almost 30 pounds of cherries are distilled to make each liter of liquor, before a long aging period. Pass over inexpensive, artificially flavored kirsch and get a bottle of the real thing, as it keeps for years.

MOCCHACCINO TORTE

Makes 10 to 12 servings

With an espresso-chocolate filling on a brownie crust, topped with airy whipped cream, this indulgent dessert has a flavor combination that you will recognize from the mocha drinks that you might find at your local coffee bar. It's a luscious chilled torte that calls for bracing cups of coffee to balance the sweetness.

CRUST

Softened unsalted butter for the pan

¾ cup all-purpose flour

½ cup (2 ounces) coarsely chopped pecans

3 tablespoons light brown sugar

2 tablespoons Dutch-processed or
natural cocoa powder

Pinch of salt

4 tablespoons (½ stick) unsalted butter, chilled,
cut into tablespoons

2 teaspoons vegetable oil

½ teaspoon vanilla extract

FILLING

4 ounces unsweetened chocolate, finely
chopped

1 cup (2 sticks) unsalted butter, at
room temperature

1 cup packed light brown sugar, rubbed
through a wire sieve to remove any lumps

2 tablespoons cold brewed espresso or
2 teaspoons instant espresso powder, dissolved
in 2 tablespoons boiling water, cooled

6 large eggs, at room temperature (see Note)

TOPPING

1¼ cups heavy cream

2 tablespoons confectioners' sugar

1¼ teaspoons instant espresso powder or
2 teaspoons regular instant coffee

1. Position a rack in the center of the oven and preheat to 350°F. Lightly butter the inside of a 9-inch springform pan.

2. To make the crust, pulse the flour, pecans, brown sugar, cocoa, and salt together in a food processor fitted with the metal chopping blade about 8 times until the pecans are finely chopped, but not a powder. Add the butter and pulse about 12 times until the mixture resembles coarse meal. Mix the vegetable oil with 2 teaspoons ice water and the vanilla. Pour over the flour mixture and pulse a few times, just until the mixture begins to clump together.

3. Press the crust firmly and evenly into the bottom of the pan. Pierce all over with a fork. Bake until the crust looks dry, about 15 minutes. Transfer the pan to a wire cake rack and let cool completely.

4. To make the filling, melt the chocolate in the top part of a double boiler over hot, not simmering, water. Remove from the heat and let cool until tepid, but pourable.

5. Beat the butter and brown sugar in a medium bowl with an electric mixer at high speed until light in color and texture, about 3 minutes. Beat in the cooled chocolate and espresso. One at a time, beat in the eggs, beating well after each addition. Pour into the cooled crust and smooth the top. Refrigerate until the filling is firm, at least 2 hours.

6. To make the topping, combine the cream, confectioners' sugar, and instant espresso in a medium bowl. Refrigerate until the espresso softens, about 15 minutes. Whip with an electric mixer on high speed until stiff. Spread evenly over the filling.

7. To serve, remove the sides of the pan. Cut with a thin knife dipped into hot water before making each slice. Serve chilled.

NOTE: This recipe contains raw eggs, which should not be served to the elderly or very young, or people with compromised immune systems.

HAZELNUT GÂTEAU WITH
COFFEE BUTTERCREAM

Makes 10 servings

This classic cake, with toasty nut flavor in every bite, is just the sweet you might have at a French café with an afternoon coffee. It is made in the time-honored French manner: spongy génoise cake layers, soaked with liqueur-spiked syrup, frosted with a rich buttercream. This buttercream, made with a base of egg whites, is one of the easiest and best around.

HAZELNUT GÉNOISE

4 tablespoons (½ stick) unsalted butter

1 teaspoon vanilla extract

1 cup cake flour (not self-rising)

⅓ cup (1½ ounces) toasted, skinned, and coarsely chopped hazelnuts (see Note)

½ teaspoon baking powder

¼ teaspoon salt

1 cup sugar

6 large eggs

FRANGELICO SYRUP

⅔ cup sugar

⅓ cup hazelnut liqueur, such as Frangelico, or use hazelnut syrup for beverages

COFFEE BUTTERCREAM

4 large egg whites

1 cup sugar

1 pound unsalted butter, at cool room temperature

3 tablespoons cold brewed espresso or 4 teaspoons instant espresso powder dissolved in 3 tablespoons boiling water and cooled

1 cup (4 ounces) toasted and skinned hazelnuts (see Note)

10 chocolate-covered espresso beans

1. Position a rack in the center of the oven and preheat to 350°F. Line the bottom of a 9-inch springform pan with a round of parchment or wax paper. Do not butter or flour the pan.

2. Melt the butter in a small, heavy-bottomed saucepan over medium heat, and let boil until the milk solids in the bottom of the pan turn light brown, 2 to 3 minutes. Remove from the heat and let stand for 1 minute. Skim the foam from the top of the butter. Carefully pour the browned butter into a medium bowl, leaving the browned milk solids behind in the saucepan. Add the vanilla.

3. Process the flour, hazelnuts, baking powder, and salt together in a food processor fitted with the metal chopping blade until the nuts are ground into a powder, about 30 seconds. Set aside.

4. Bring a medium saucepan with 1 inch of water to a brisk simmer over high heat. Reduce the heat to medium-low to maintain the simmer. Whisk the sugar and eggs together in the bowl of a heavy-duty standing mixer. Place over the water (the bowl should not touch the water) and whisk constantly until the sugar is dissolved and the egg mixture is hot (dip in your finger), about 2 minutes. Attach the bowl to the mixer and fit with the whisk attachment. Beat on high speed until the mixture is very pale and fluffy and has tripled in volume, about 4 minutes. (Another test: Stop the mixer and lift the whisk attachment. The mixture should form a thick ribbon that falls back on itself and stays on the surface for a few seconds before sinking. Professional bakers call this "making the ribbon.") You can use a large heatproof bowl and a hand mixer to prepare the egg mixture, but allow at least 5 minutes of beating.

5. Remove the bowl from the mixer. In thirds, sprinkle the flour mixture over the egg mixture and fold it in with a large balloon whisk or a rubber spatula. Transfer about one-fourth of the batter to the butter-vanilla mixture and whisk together to combine. Return this mixture to the batter and fold it in. Pour into the pan and smooth the top.

6. Bake until the top of the cake springs back when lightly pressed in the center with your fingers, about 35 minutes. Let cool in the pan on a wire cake rack for 10 minutes. Run a sharp knife around the inside of the pan to release the cake. Invert the cake onto the rack and remove the pan bottom and parchment. Turn right side up and let cool completely.

7. To make the syrup, combine the sugar and ¾ cup water in a medium saucepan. Bring to a boil over medium heat, stirring to dissolve the sugar. Stop stirring and boil for 1 minute. Remove from the heat and let cool. Stir in the liqueur.

8. To make the buttercream, bring a medium saucepan with 1 inch of water to a brisk simmer over high heat. Reduce the heat to medium-low to maintain the simmer. Combine the egg whites and sugar in a very clean bowl of a heavy-duty standing mixer. Place over the water (the bowl should not touch the water) and whisk constantly until the sugar is dissolved and the egg mixture is opaque white and hot (dip in your finger), about 2 minutes. Attach the bowl to the mixer and fit with the whisk attachment. Beat on high speed until stiff, shiny peaks form and the meringue is cool, about 6 minutes. (You can use a large heatproof bowl and a hand mixer to prepare the meringue. After heating the egg whites mixture, place the bowl on a wire cake rack to allow better air circulation to cool the mixture, and allow at least 8 minutes of beating.)

9. One tablespoon at a time, beat in the butter and continue beating until the buttercream is smooth and fluffy. Beat in the espresso.

10. To assemble the cake, using a long serrated knife, cut the cake in half horizontally. Place the top layer (with the "skin"), cut side up, on a 9-inch cardboard cake round. Brush half of the syrup over the cake layer. Spread with about ½ cup of the buttercream. Top with the remaining cake layer, cut side down. Brush with the remaining syrup. Spread the top, then the sides, with a thin layer of buttercream. Refrigerate the cake until the buttercream is set, about 10 minutes.

11. Transfer about ¾ cup of the buttercream to a pastry bag fitted with a ½-inch star tip, such as Ateco #825. Spread the top and then the sides of the cake with the remaining buttercream. Pipe 10 equally spaced rosettes around the top perimeter of the cake. Press handfuls of the chopped hazelnuts around the sides and over the top of the cake. Place an espresso bean in each rosette. Place the cake on a serving platter. (The cake can be made up to 1 day ahead, covered with a cake dome and stored at room temperature.) Slice and serve.

NOTE: To toast hazelnuts, spread the nuts on a rimmed baking sheet. Bake in a preheated 350°F oven until the skins are cracked and the nut flesh is golden brown, 12 to 15 minutes. Wrap the nuts in a clean kitchen towel and let stand until cool enough to handle. Using the towel, rub the skins off the nuts. Don't worry about removing every last shred of skin.

CHOCOLATE-STRAWBERRY SACHERTORTE

Makes 10 servings

While researching my book *Kaffeehaus*, I collected many recipes for Sachertorte, which just might be the ultimate Viennese coffeehouse dessert. The Viennese like their Sachertorte without frills—just a dense chocolate cake with a shiny chocolate glaze (really a thin fudge, and none too easy to make) and a big dollop of whipped cream. This authentic approach is sometimes too austere for American tastes, so here's a somewhat simplified version that uses strawberries to bring the components together. And don't skip the whipped cream, which is really needed to moisten the firm cake.

CAKE

5 ounces semisweet chocolate (no more than 62% cacao), finely chopped

9 tablespoons (1 stick plus 1 tablespoon) unsalted butter, at cool room temperature, plus more for the pan

1 cup confectioners' sugar

6 large eggs, separated, at room temperature

1 teaspoon vanilla extract

½ cup granulated sugar

1 cup all-purpose flour, plus more for the pan

¼ teaspoon fine sea salt

1 cup strawberry preserves (not sugarless)

CHOCOLATE GLAZE

⅔ cup heavy cream

6 ounces semisweet chocolate (no more than 62% cacao), finely chopped

2 tablespoons light corn syrup

10 large strawberries with stems for garnish

Sweetened whipped cream for garnish

1. Position a rack in the center of the oven and preheat to 350°F. Lightly butter the inside of a 9-inch springform pan. Line the bottom with a round of wax paper. Dust the inside of the pan with flour and tap out the excess.

2. To make the cake, melt the chocolate in the top part of a double boiler set over hot, not simmering, water. Remove the insert from the heat and let the chocolate cool until tepid but still pourable, about 10 minutes.

3. Beat the butter and confectioners' sugar in a medium bowl with an electric mixer set on low speed until the mixture is combined, about 1 minute. Increase the speed to high and beat, occasionally scraping down the sides of the bowl, until light in color and texture, about 3 minutes. Beat in the chocolate. One at a time, beat in the egg yolks, again scraping down the sides of the bowl as needed, then the vanilla. Reduce the mixer speed to low and beat in the granulated sugar, flour, and salt.

4. Using clean beaters, beat the whites in a medium bowl with an electric mixer set on high speed just until soft peaks form. Stir one-fourth of the whites into the chocolate batter to lighten the mixture, then fold in the remaining whites. Spread evenly in the pan.

5. Bake until a wooden toothpick inserted in the center of the cake comes out clean, about 45 minutes. Let cool on a wire cake rack for 10 minutes. Remove the sides of the pan. Invert the cake onto the rack and remove the pan bottom and wax paper. Invert again so the top of the cake faces up and let cool completely.

6. Bring the preserves and 1 tablespoon water to a boil over medium heat, stirring often. Boil for 1 minute. Strain through a wire sieve into a small bowl and press firmly on the solids in the sieve. Discard the solids. Let the strawberry glaze cool slightly.

7. If the top of the cake has domed, trim off the domed part with a serrated knife so that the top is flat. Discard the cake trimmings. Place the cake on the wire rack on a rimmed baking sheet. Pour the strawberry glaze over the top of the cake, being sure to fill any small holes in the cake with the glaze. Smooth the glaze over the top of the cake with an offset metal spatula, letting the excess run down the sides. Use the spatula to pick up the glaze on the baking sheet and spread onto any unglazed areas of the cake. Let cool until the glaze has set, about 30 minutes.

8. To make the chocolate glaze, bring the cream to a boil in a small saucepan over medium heat. Remove from the heat and add the chocolate. Let stand until the chocolate softens, about 3 minutes. Add the corn syrup and stir with a rubber spatula until the chocolate is melted and the mixture is smooth. (Do not whisk, as this creates air bubbles that will mar the surface of the glaze.) Let cool until slightly thickened but still liquid and pourable, about 20 minutes.

9. Transfer the cake on the rack to a clean rimmed baking sheet. Pour the chocolate glaze over the top of the cake and smooth the glaze with an offset metal spatula, letting the excess run down the sides. Use the spatula to pick up the glaze on the baking sheet and spread onto any unglazed areas of the cake. Place the stemmed strawberries around the top perimeter of the cake. Refrigerate until the glaze has set, about 30 minutes. (The cake can be made up to 1 day ahead. Remove from the refrigerator 30 minutes before serving.) Using a sharp knife dipped in hot water and dried between each slice, cut the cake into wedges. Serve, with a large dollop of whipped cream next to each slice.

STICKY TOFFEE PUDDING

Makes 8 servings

Lovers of warm, gooey desserts will swoon over this British contribution to the genre. It is not an American pudding, but a warm, mildly spiced date cake moistened by warm toffee sauce. Don't be concerned about the unusual addition of baking soda to the soaking dates, as it helps soften them. Be sure to serve it with ice cream or whipped cream.

TOFFEE SAUCE

1 cup sugar

¼ cup water

1 tablespoon light corn syrup

2 cups heavy cream, heated until steaming

2 tablespoons unsalted butter

1 teaspoon vanilla extract

DATE CAKE

1 cup pitted and diced (½-inch) dates

1 cup water

1 teaspoon instant espresso powder

1 teaspoon baking soda

1¼ cups all-purpose flour

1 teaspoon baking powder

½ teaspoon ground ginger

½ teaspoon salt

¾ cup sugar

4 tablespoons (½ stick) unsalted butter, at room temperature

2 large eggs, beaten, at room temperature

1 teaspoon vanilla extract

Vanilla ice cream or sweetened whipped cream for serving

1. To make the toffee sauce, combine the sugar, water, and corn syrup in a heavy-bottomed medium saucepan. Cook over high heat, stirring constantly, until boiling. Stop stirring and cook, occasionally swirling the saucepan by the handle, until the mixture is deep amber, smoking, and has a sharp aroma (see Note). Reduce the heat to low. Gradually stir in the hot cream and butter (take care, as the toffee will bubble furiously) and stir until smooth. Remove from the heat and cool slightly. Stir in the vanilla. Let cool until warm.

2. Position a rack in the center of the oven and preheat to 350°F. Lightly butter, but do not flour, an 8 x 11½-inch baking pan. Spread ½ cup of the toffee sauce in the pan and refrigerate while making the batter. Reserve the remaining toffee sauce at room temperature.

3. To make the cake, bring the dates and water to a boil in a medium saucepan over medium heat. Cook, stirring occasionally, until the dates are soft and the liquid is reduced to ½ cup, about 5 minutes. Remove from the heat and stir in the espresso powder, then the baking soda (the mixture will bubble). Transfer the saucepan to a bowl of ice water and let cool until tepid.

4. Sift the flour, baking powder, ginger, and salt together in a medium bowl. Beat the sugar and butter together in another medium bowl with an electric mixer on high speed until the mixture is light in color, about 2 minutes. Gradually beat in the beaten eggs, then the vanilla. Reduce the mixer speed to low. In thirds, alternating with two equal additions of the date mixture, beat in the flour mixture until combined, occasionally scraping down the sides of the bowl. Spread the batter evenly over the toffee sauce in the pan.

5. Bake until a wooden toothpick inserted in the center of the cake comes out clean, about 30 minutes.

6. If needed, reheat the toffee sauce until warm. Remove the cake from the oven and pierce all over with the tines of a meat fork. Spread ½ cup of the toffee sauce over the top of the cake and let stand until the cake absorbs the sauce, about 5 minutes.

7. Using a large serving spoon, scoop the warm cake into individual serving bowls. Top each with the warm sauce and add a scoop of ice cream. Serve at once.

NOTE: When making toffee from granulated sugar (as opposed to brown sugar), rely on your eyes and nose to tell you when it's done. If the syrup is merely cooked until it is light brown, the flavor will not have the distinctive toffee notes, so be bold. The color should be deep amber brown, a few shades darker than a new penny. Smoke is a sign that the temperature is high enough to change the melted sugar into toffee, so don't be alarmed. Finally, the toffee should give off a sharp, but not burned, aroma.

TIRAMISÙ CAKE WITH MASCARPONE FROSTING

Makes 10 servings

Tiramisù may be standard at Italian-American bakeries and cafés, but it has, surprisingly, not been around forever. It can be traced back only to the 1970s and a restaurant in Treviso. The heavenly combination of Italian ladyfingers, Marsala, espresso, and mascarpone usually makes an unassuming, even dowdy-looking dessert. This version upgrades the ingredients into a beautiful cake. Bring out the demitasse cups and pour strong Italian roast coffee with this showstopper.

CAKE

4 tablespoons (½ stick) unsalted butter

1 teaspoon vanilla extract

1 cup granulated sugar

6 large eggs

1 cup cake flour (not self-rising)

¼ teaspoon salt

ESPRESSO SYRUP

½ cup granulated sugar

½ cup water

⅓ cup brewed Italian or French roast coffee or espresso, or 3 tablespoons instant espresso powder, dissolved in ⅓ cup boiling water, cooled

⅓ cup sweet Marsala

1¼ cups chilled heavy cream

One 17-ounce container mascarpone cheese

3 tablespoons confectioners' sugar

1 ounce semisweet or bittersweet chocolate

1. Position a rack in the center of the oven and preheat to 350°F. Line the bottom of a 9-inch springform pan with a round of parchment or wax paper. Do not butter or flour the pan.

2. To make the cake, melt the butter in a small, heavy-bottomed saucepan over medium heat and let boil until the milk solids in the bottom of the pan turn light brown, about 1½ minutes. Remove from the heat and let stand for 1 minute. Skim the foam from the top of the butter. Carefully pour the browned butter into a medium bowl, leaving the browned milk solids behind in the saucepan. Add the vanilla.

3. Bring a medium saucepan with 1 inch of water to a brisk simmer over high heat. Reduce the heat to medium-low to maintain the simmer. Whisk the sugar and eggs together in the bowl of a heavy-duty standing mixer. Place over the water (the bowl should not touch the water) and whisk constantly until the sugar is dissolved and the egg mixture is hot (dip in your finger), about 2 minutes. Attach the bowl to the mixer and fit with the whisk attachment. Beat on high speed until the mixture is very pale and fluffy and has tripled in volume, about 4 minutes. (Another test: Stop the mixer and lift the whisk attachment. The mixture should form a thick ribbon that falls back on itself and stays on the surface for a few seconds before sinking. Professional bakers call this "making the ribbon.") You can use a large heatproof bowl and a hand mixer to prepare the egg mixture, but allow at least 5 minutes of beating.

4. Remove the bowl from the mixer. Sift the flour and salt together and return to the sieve or sifter. In thirds, sprinkle the flour mixture over the egg mixture and fold it in with a large balloon whisk or a rubber spatula. Transfer about one-fourth of the batter to the butter-vanilla mixture and whisk together to combine. Return this mixture to the batter and fold it in. Pour into the pan and smooth the top.

5. Bake until the top of the cake springs back when lightly pressed in the center with your fingers, about 35 minutes. Let cool in the pan on a wire cake rack for 10 minutes. Run a sharp knife around the inside of the pan to release the cake. Invert the cake onto the rack and remove the pan bottom and wax paper. Turn right side up and let cool completely.

6. To make the syrup, combine the sugar and water in a medium saucepan. Bring to a boil over medium heat, stirring to dissolve the sugar. Stop stirring and boil for 1 minute. Remove from the heat. Stir in the coffee and Marsala. Let cool.

7. To assemble the cake, whip 1 cup of the heavy cream in a chilled bowl with an electric mixer on high speed until it forms soft peaks. In another bowl, whisk the mascarpone, confectioners'

sugar, and remaining ¼ cup cream just until smooth. Do not overmix. Add to the whipped cream and whip just until combined and stiff enough to spread.

8. Using a long serrated knife, cut the cake in half horizontally. Place the top layer (with the "skin"), cut side up, on a 9-inch cardboard cake round. Brush half of the syrup over the cake layer. Spread with about ½ cup of the mascarpone frosting. Top with the remaining cake layer, cut side down. Brush with the remaining syrup. Spread the top, then the sides, with the remaining frosting.

9. Grate the chocolate on the large holes of a box grater into a small bowl. Sprinkle the grated chocolate over the top of the cake. (Do not touch the chocolate with your fingers or it will melt.) Place the cake on a serving platter. Refrigerate until the frosting is set, about 1 hour. (The cake can refrigerated for up to 2 days.) Slice and serve.

SOURCES

The amount of information on coffee online is staggering.
Here are some of my favorite sites for both bakery supplies and all things coffee.

Amazon
www.amazon.com

The kitchenware and grocery stores at this online giant keep getting better and better. You will find all kinds of coffeemakers here, as well as implements to make Thai and Vietnamese coffee.

The Coffee Review
www.coffeereview.com

Not a commercial site, but a fascinating review of various coffee beans from around the world. Their list of sponsors is a Who's Who of the American coffee business.

Pastry Sampler
Beach Cuisine, Inc.
1672 Main Street, STE E, #159
Ramona, CA 92065
(760) 440-9171
www.pastrysampler.com

One-stop shopping for all professional-quality baking supplies, this online store is where you'll find a wide assortment of pastry tips.

Sur La Table
Box 840
Brownsburg, IN 46112
(800) 243-0852
www.surlatable.com

With more than seventy well-stocked stores nationwide, and a great online shop, you are likely to find what you are looking for at this top-notch kitchenware supplier.

Sweet Maria's Coffee
1115 21st Street
Oakland, CA 94609
www.sweetmarias.com

After checking out this encyclopedic site, you may feel that, as far as top-notch coffee is concerned, if they don't have it, it doesn't exist. It is also an invaluable source for coffee information with a very personal slant.

Williams-Sonoma
3250 Van Ness Avenue
San Francisco, CA 94109
(877) 812-6235
www.williams-sonoma.com

The kitchenware and tabletop giant sells top-of-the-line baking supplies from half-sheet pans to food coloring.

INDEX

Note: *Italicized* page references indicate photographs.